AMERICAN HEROES

ROGER WILLIAMS
ABRAHAM LINCOLN
HARRIET TUBMAN
CLARA BARTON

BARBOUR
PUBLISHING, INC.
Uhrichsville, Ohio

© 2001 by Barbour Publishing, Inc.

ISBN 1-58660-132-6

Roger Williams by Mark Ammerman. © 1995 by Barbour Publishing, Inc.
Abraham Lincoln by Sam Wellman. © 1985 by Barbour Publishing, Inc.
Harriet Tubman by Callie Smith Grant. © 1999 by Barbour Publishing, Inc.
Clara Barton by David R. Collins. © 1999 by Barbour Publishing, Inc.

All Scripture quotations are taken from the King James Version of the Bible.

Published by Barbour Publishing, Inc., P.O. Box 719, Uhrichsville, Ohio 44683
http://www.barbourbooks.com

ecpa Member of the
Evangelical Christian
Publishers Association

Printed in the United States of America.

CONTENTS

ROGER WILLIAMS

FRIEND OF THE PERSECUTED

by Mark Ammerman

INTRODUCTION

Imagine a world without TV, McDonald's packaged snacks, cars, bicycles, roller blades, microwaves, electric lights, hot showers, aspirin, deodorant, sneakers, T-shirts, contact lenses, computers, telephones, machine guns, or nuclear missiles.

Imagine a nation where only one kind of church is legal and where it is dangerous to say that you believe in something different. Where the law says you must go to church each Sunday and where the king or queen or bishop tells everyone how to live. Where people can be thrown into prison for the wrong reasons without any trial. Where the government takes your money whenever it wants to. Where school lasts from sunup to suppertime, if you get to go at all. Where books are only allowed if the king's book-checker says so.

This is the world of Roger Williams as a boy. This is England in the beginning of the seventeenth century.

But people then were not much different than they are today. They worked and played and laughed and prayed, just like we do. They went to see Shakespeare's plays in theaters. They enjoyed live musical concerts, or they made music themselves and sang together to pass the time. They told stories. They watched puppet shows and parades and went to fairs. They played cards, ran in races, and had other competitions. They went out to eat and drink at inns or at the homes of friends. Sometimes everyone was invited to a feast at the house of some rich man. They made their own fresh bread or bought it from others who made it. They made pies and cakes and candies. They drank tea and milk. When they traveled long distances, they walked or rode horses or donkeys. Sometimes they rode on wagons or carriages pulled by animals, or in ships or boats. They built buildings as tall as they could and bridges as long as they could. They used wood and stone and brick and metal and glass. They built stoves and ovens or cooked over fires, and they used salt and ice to preserve foods. They had doctors and dentists. They made clothes by hand and enjoyed various fashions. They sent letters by messengers or by friends who were traveling. Soldiers were sometimes policemen and sometimes armies. They used muskets, swords, pikes, bows and arrows, and cannons. They marched or rode on horses.

Even with only one legal church in England, some people still had the courage to worship God differently. Some people still preached about Jesus even when the church told them not to. Many people knew the Bible and loved the Lord. Many people began to believe that God would help them to rule their own country without a king. Many people tried to start good laws that gave others rights that could be protected. Some people went to school and then to college. They studied math and the Bible and different languages. There were books and pamphlets for those who could read. The King James Bible was first published during this time, and many good Christian books were available.

The capital of England was London. Roger Williams was born there. It was a very big, very crowded, very busy city, full of buildings and people and animals. Even London Bridge had houses and stores built upon it. The king lived in London, too, and all the offices of his government were there.

In the countryside, the farms of the poor, the estates of the rich, and the little towns of the villagers were very busy, too.

Now, imagine a world where there are tall trees and clear rivers that go on and on for endless miles. Under those trees are wild animals of all kinds and people who live in tents and houses made of poles and bark and animal hides. They have no clothes except small coverings of animal skins, and all they have for cooking and hunting is made of wood, stone, bone, or shells from the rivers and seas. They plant corn and a few other vegetables. They hunt and fish and go to war. They cook over open fires. Their homes are heated the same way, and there is a hole in the roof to let out the smoke. They drink water. They sometimes kill and eat each other. They fight with knives and spears and clubs and bows and arrows. They believe in many different false gods and spirits, and live in fear of them all. They don't know who Jesus is, and Satan has them bound in darkness. When they are sick, their doctors make medicines from things that grow; and the doctors try to convince the spirits to take the sickness away. They have sachems (kings) who rule over them, and they have laws and customs that they pass down from generation to generation. Boys and girls grow up to be just like their parents in everything. They have no schools and no books. But even though life is often cruel and hard, they have a natural love for their families and friends. They laugh and they play. They tell stories and sing songs. They have races and competitions.

These people are the Indians of the great northeastern forests of America. They have lived this way for a long time.

On the edge of these savage forests, along the shore of the Atlantic Ocean, stand a handful of small English villages surrounded by walls made of wood from the trees of the forest. Soldiers with muskets and cannons guard the walls. There are a few nice houses in each village, but most are not much better than the homes of the Indians. They are furnished with items brought from England. In every village there is a church or meetinghouse where the people gather to worship the Lord. The town is ruled by magistrates and a governor who are elected by the members of the church. Food is scarce, and the people have to hunt and farm and fish like the Indians. Often they trade their English tools and trinkets for food from the natives. Sometimes another ship comes from across the ocean, bringing supplies and more people. Life is much harder than it was in England. There is much sickness and death. There is much sorrow and longing for things that are old and familiar. But the people are quickly learning how to live in this New World. And above all, they are learning to truly trust God. So there is much joy, as well—deep joy amidst the pain and hardship of life in the wilderness. Sometimes they are able to share the gospel of Jesus Christ with their Indian neighbors. Some of the Indians have begun to believe in the true God.

This was the world of Roger Williams when he was twenty-seven years old. This was America in 1630.

CHAPTER 1

1611

The morning dawned as many other winter days in the bustling London suburb of West Smithfield. Before the sun rose or the cock crowed, hundreds of stoves in hundreds of cold, crowded wooden houses had been fired up against the damp March morning. Already at 5:00 A.M., the streets were filling up with the activity of a long, noisy day of business and play.

The year was 1611, and on Cow Lane—a narrow, winding street in the busy center of London's merchant district—an eight-year-old boy peered down from his third-story bedroom window at his waking neighborhood. His thick, dark hair was tousled and matted from a fitful night's sleep, but his thoughtful brown eyes were keenly awake as he surveyed the sights in the avenue below.

Down the crooked lane, men and women faded in and out of the morning mist, as if in a dream. Some bore large woven baskets or burden-filled bags. Some carried satchels of papers or bundles of cloth. Some pushed wheelbarrows or rode carts pulled by donkeys. The muffled sounds of morning greetings could be heard amidst the patter and clatter of foot and hoof and wheel on cobblestone. Shop doors opened and closed as merchants began to haul out their wares for display.

Two stories directly below our young observer, James Williams—merchant taylor, buyer and seller of cloth— unlatched his own shop door and stepped out into the foggy

Smithfield air. As he briskly started across the street, he suddenly stopped. Turning around, his gaze went upward toward the living quarters above his shop, and his eyes met those of his eight year old.

"Good morning, Roger!" shouted Mr. Williams.

The boy pushed open his window a crack. "Good morning, Father."

"Roger, rouse your brothers if they aren't already up! Get dressed and have your breakfasts. We've work to do this day."

Then James Williams turned again and continued across the street and through the door of St. George's Inn. There, as was his habit each morning, he would hear any news of the night past and talk of the day ahead.

But there was something very unusual about this morning. There were many unfamiliar faces in the inn. There were many strangers in the street. More women and children than usual. More donkeys and horses. More talk.

The scene from Roger's window was beginning to resemble the jumbled mass of party goers who flocked to Smithfield once a year for St. Bartholomew's Fair. But this crowd was not a festive one. There was something in the faces of the people—something in the way they moved and spoke with each other—that evidenced troubled opinions and worrisome fears. Roger could see anger. Sorrow. Confusion.

"Today is the burning," said Roger aloud as he turned toward his brothers, both already putting on their clothing.

"Today is the burning," echoed six-year-old Robert absently as he tied his shoes.

"Yes, but that's not 'til noon," replied Sydrach, Roger's elder by three years. "We've plenty to do helping Mother and Father 'til then."

But it turned out that there was very little to do that morning, for folks were more intent on talk than work. The more the streets filled, the more the people talked.

James Williams's shop was packed that morning with a small, sober group of men, all of whom Roger knew as friends of his father. All were merchant taylors like his father, and members of London's Merchant Taylors' Company. But they weren't discussing business. Roger and Sydrach sat on boxes in the back of the shop and listened.

"Legate is a heretic—the worst of his kind. It makes no difference that he's a fellow merchant taylor. He deserves to burn for his poisonous teachings!" declared a Mr. Fuller with a violent shake of his long grey hair and his thick, drooping mustache.

"He's a heretic, yes," agreed a Mr. Finch, whose clear blue eyes peered round about at his colleagues in the room. "And to preach that Christ is not God and not to be prayed to is poison indeed!"

Many heads nodded in sad agreement.

"But," continued Mr. Finch, "to turn a man into a torch for his opinions is just too. . ."

"Opinions, indeed!" interrupted Fuller with a sudden wave of his arm. "There is God's truth, and there is the devil's falsehood! There is true doctrine, and there is heresy! The Church of England declares the doctrines of God, and we are to hold them to our hearts or perish in our sins!"

"I go along with the bit about God and the devil, but some of us fellows hold a different opinion in some matters than the Church of England, Mr. Fuller," said a Mr. Smythe quietly.

"Some of you Puritan fellows put too much on a man's right to hold an opinion!" shouted Fuller.

"Opinions aside for a bit. Let's talk about the man," said Finch. "Two years ago when my shop burned, Legate sold me a quarter of his wares at no profit to himself. And all to help me back on my feet."

"And when my little Sally died," added a Mr. Johnson, sorrowfully and thoughtfully, "Bartholomew Legate was the first to come and pray with me. Though who he was prayin' to I guess I don't now know."

"And he was always first to speak well for the Merchant Taylors' Company, wasn't he?" furthered Smythe. "When Parliament forced us to help pay for colonization in Virginia, Legate sweetened it for us by getting them to promise one hundred acres of Virginia land to every contributor who had a trade."

"So, for which of these fine acts of citizenship and friendship does he stand condemned today?" challenged Roger's father.

"For none of these, Father!" spoke a young voice from behind the band of businessmen. It was Sydrach.

"For none of these but for heresy, Father," said Sydrach with conviction and yet with fear. "Mother says heresy is a sickness that spreads. And like a fire in a stable, it must be quickly quenched. Mr. Legate won't be quiet, and he won't quit, so his candle must be put out."

"Sydrach!" exploded his father. "For all our talk of free opinions, I will have yours—and your mother's—in private from now on!"

The men laughed, but the boy shrank at his father's

words. As he turned his head to the floor, his eyes became defiant.

James Williams continued to rail at his oldest son. "This candle you would rashly put out has burned warmly and kindly at our own table for years, Sydrach! He has been a welcomed guest in this home since before your birth! He prayed over you in your own cradle, long before he took it upon himself to dethrone Christ! Above all, though I hate his heresy for the heresy it is, he has been a friend!

"A friend," he quietly repeated, more to himself than to Sydrach. "A true friend."

And here Mr. Williams turned suddenly away from Sydrach, walked quickly from the circle of men, sat down upon a heap of cloth, covered his face with his hands, and began to weep.

Roger had so seldom seen his father cry that he instantly ran to him and threw his arms around him. Sydrach stood up and, without looking at the men, left the room.

As the hour of the burning approached, all Smithfield (and a good deal of the rest of London) moved as one body through the parish of St. Sepulchre's toward the appointed place of execution.

James Williams and his family (his wife Alice, their oldest child Catherine, and their three sons) pressed forward in the crowd as far as they could safely go together. James, instructing the family to stick together where they were, pushed onward to where he caught sight of his friend, Bartholomew Legate. The condemned man was tied to a stake and surrounded by brush and wood.

"My goodness, Legate!" cried James above the deafening

mob. "Call on the Savior even now! He hears! He truly hears!"

But Legate's own ears, cut off in partial punishment for his heresy, could not hear his colleague's admonition. As James stared upon the scene in disbelief and horror, Roger slipped silently beside him. He had followed his father through the forest of arms and legs, and he reached now for his hand.

The moment had come, and the noise of the crowd quieted to the intermittent barking of dogs and the crying of babies. The charges of heresy were read, the sentence was pronounced, and the fire was lit. A mournful gasp escaped the crowd as though an eerie wind had suddenly filled the church courtyard, and the prayers of the burning man could be heard rising with the crackling flames. The heat of the fire and the brilliance of the noonday sun, with the growing roar of the deadly flames and the groaning crowd made Roger dizzy. His father took him in his arms, and from this vantage point the young boy watched Bartholomew Legate die.

As the blackened form of the condemned man melted and collapsed within the center of the consuming pyre, Roger could bear it no more. "Mr. Legate! Mr. Legate! Mr. Legate!" he sobbed as he buried his face in his father's cloak.

Mr. Legate had often carried Roger on his shoulders through these very streets. He had eaten and laughed and prayed at his father's table. He had sat Roger upon his lap and read to him from his father's Bible. In fact—and this was the memory that brought the bitterest tears—it was in those readings from the Scriptures that Roger's young heart had been turned toward Jesus, had opened wide, had believed. And yet this man no longer believed that Jesus was God, and so the fires of hell had broken loose from beneath the earth in

Smithfield and consumed him. But no! These were not hell's flames. This fire was lit by man, and set to man, to kill a man. Did Jesus, Who died for all, ever command such a thing? Roger was sure He had not.

As the crowd began to wander away into the streets and alleys of Smithfield, Roger and his father returned to their waiting family. Together they walked slowly and silently toward their home on Cow Lane.

Roger was the first to break the silence. "Father, should a good man be killed for having bad ideas?"

"Hush, Roger!" said his mother. "Mr. Legate denied the Lord's deity. He was fool enough to teach others his bad ideas. And now God is his judge."

"God will indeed be his judge, Alice, and I fear for the foolish man's soul. But man was his judge this day," countered James. "The church was his judge. The king was his judge."

"Should not the king judge heretics, Father?" asked Sydrach, with a trace of a challenge in his voice.

James ignored the challenge but offered one of his own, "What if the king were a heretic, Son? Who would judge him?"

"James!" fired Alice.

"Is the king a heretic, Father?" asked Roger.

"I did not say so. Only that he is not God," replied Mr. Williams.

At home, Roger pulled a book from his father's shelf and laid it open upon the kitchen table. It was *Foxe's Book of Martyrs,* a volume filled with stories and pictures of men and women who had been martyred for their faith in Christ. Judged and killed by kings and queens and bishops, most of them had been executed for simply believing something different than the kings and queens and bishops had told them to believe. Many of them had died right there in Smithfield, only a half century before Roger was born.

He turned the familiar pages—pages known to all men, women, boys, and girls in England in those days—until he came to the story of a man named John Lambert. Lambert was burned at Smithfield in 1538, during the reign of Henry VII. The picture on the page showed Lambert tied to the stake with the flames ascending. Lifting his burning hands, he was crying out, "None but Christ. None but Christ!"

CHAPTER 2

1612

"Captain Smith and the Indians. After school at the docks," whispered Roger to his schoolmate, Jon.

It was almost time for the 3:30 afternoon break, but that would be brief, and the 5:00 dismissal seemed like days away to the boys (Anthony Pigs, they were called) at St. Anthony's School on Threadneedle Street. The warm June sun tempted all the little "pigs" to thoughts far more adventurous than to master the ancient Latin grammar. Languages fascinated Roger, but he wanted more to be dreaming and playing along the riverside with his Dutch friend.

When school finally let out, Roger Williams and Jon Vanderhook ran through the crowded streets toward the docks in Smithfield on the River Thames. There were the ships with their tall masts and their cargoes from faraway worlds. There were the hovering gulls that swam upon the breezes like the boats upon the water. There too were the sailors with their many strange accents and their captivating tales of life upon the treacherous sea.

"Right here!" declared Roger as he stood upon the wooden wharf. "This is where Captain John Smith got off his ship on his return from the New World—all the way from Virginia beyond the seas!"

"Can you imagine what it's like over there?" continued Roger excitedly. "The deep ocean and the wild forests. Fiercely painted Indians in their homes in the woods. Mighty rivers that lie beneath tall trees and stretch on and on forever."

"All that and no London Bridge!" said Jon.

"All that and no king's castles!" added Roger.

"All that and no Latin!" shouted Jon, and the boys laughed as they tossed bits of wood onto the wide river.

"It's all very exciting and frightening at the same time," said Jon. "But let's pretend we are there. Let's hunt for the beaches where the rubies and diamonds lie like shells on the sand."

"Father says there are no rubies," said Roger. "Only wild lands and wild hearts that need to hear the gospel. And Captain Smith, who worships where my family does at St. Sepulchre's, says that we are wrong to cross the seas for gold or greed."

The boys sat down for a moment on the edge of the dock, legs dangling over the slow-moving waters of the dark Thames. Their minds wandered from the busy London riverside to a lonely land beyond the horizon, a land that was fast capturing the imagination of all England. A land that seemed to hold out promises and hopes that could only be dreamed of now.

"In my church at Austin Friars," said Jon, "everybody is talking of a bay above Virginia discovered by Holland."

"A new bay?" asked Roger.

"Yes. It will be a Dutch colony, not an English one. I don't know if I'd rather go to Virginia or to this new Holland," continued Jon.

"Since you are English and Dutch, I think you should visit both," said Roger. Then he jumped up and began to pace the dock. "Let's pretend that you are the Dutch governor in that new bay, and I will be Captain Smith. Together, we'll go to visit King Powhatan, noble chief of the savage Indians.

He'll capture us, but you will escape and go for help. Then Powhatan's daughter Pocahontas will rescue me from death, just as Captain Smith has written in his book about Virginia."

"If my sister were here, she could play Pocahontas," offered Jon.

Roger made a face and said, "Aw, she's always chasin' after me! Let's not mix our fun with real girls. And we can be our own Indians, too. C'mon, let's gather some gull feathers to make Indian hair bands."

The two boys scrambled down from the dock to the wet river's edge in search of props for their fantasy. Above them, in the street that ran beside the Thames, an older group of boys was parading homeward after a swim. When Roger and Jon emerged from the shadows beneath the pier, their hair was decked with feathers, and their faces were smeared with "Indian paint" of Thames shore mud. They were waving make-believe Indian hatchets made of sticks and shouting made-up Indian war cries when they came face-to-face with the older boys.

"Ow? What 'ave we 'ere?" asked a self-appointed leader of the gang of swimmers. "Looks like some Virginia savages out for English blood!"

The gang laughed, and so did Roger, but Jon shrank back a bit.

"We're on our way to Jamestown to recapture Captain Smith," said Roger. "Do you want to play?"

The gang leader, a redheaded lad of about thirteen years, ignored Roger and stared at Jon. "Looks like this one is a Dutch savage and not a Virginian, after all. Course there's not much difference, as we can all see, right, mates?"

The older boys laughed again and pushed and ribbed each other. But Roger wasn't laughing now.

The redhead, looking straight at Jon, continued his verbal bullying. "So, little chief, just who does yer tribe worship, anyhow? The Lord A'mighty or some 'foreign god'? D' you obey the Church of England, or d' you sacrifice to demons in yer stinkin' huts?"

The bully, though it sounded as though he were poking fun at Indian paganism, was actually ridiculing the religious traditions of the Protestant Dutch community of Austin Friars (about which, since he had never been inside their church or their homes, he actually knew nothing). This group of Dutch and French families had fled to England to escape religious persecution and had obtained unique permission from the king of England to worship as they chose. But because their faith and life were different from their English neighbors, they were often made fun of, hooted at, or abused in the streets.

Roger stepped closer to the gang of jeering boys. Though he was smaller than some of them by nearly a foot, he was not afraid of them. He knew most of them by name. They were his neighbors, and some were his friends.

"Jack Dickens," said Roger to the chief bully, whom he knew to be a friend of Sydrach's and a member of his own church. "Why can't you let us alone? Reverend Edwards says the Austin Friars worship Jesus, too. They just go about it a bit different, but that's no reason to be mean to them. Jon is a Christian, and he's my friend."

But Jack Dickens was in no mood to be moved by pious reasoning.

"Ow? And if 'e's your friend, then you must be just like

'im. You're both little savages, as yer faces plainly show! 'Ere! Back to the shadowy woods with ya!" said Dickens. He gave Roger a rough shove, and the nine year old tumbled backwards over the cobblestones and fell at Jon's feet.

Jon was angry. He had been beaten before because of the faith of his family. He had run through alleys to escape many a larger bully or gang. He didn't run this time. As Roger got slowly up, rubbing a badly bruised elbow, Jon scooped up a round stone and flung it straight at Jack.

It hit him square in the head. His legs went out from under him and down he went, as though he were a wooden pin knocked over by a bowling ball. A harsh cry went up from the older boys, and several of them pounced on Jon.

"Stop it!" shouted Roger, as he tried in vain to pull the boys off his friend. "Peter! Henry! Call off your mates!" he yelled to the other boys who were still standing by. But they kept their distance from the pile of flailing arms and legs.

By the time a couple of sailors heard the ruckus and broke it up, little Jon had been badly bruised and bloodied. And Jack Dickens was still unconscious in the street. When he was finally roused, he couldn't remember who he was or how he came to have such a marvelous lump on his forehead. His friends had to walk him home. But his father soon reminded him of his fine heritage and his good name, and he was shortly well enough to carry on his mischief as before.

Roger had to convince one of the swimmers, Henry Adams, to help him carry Jon to the Vanderhook house.

As they headed toward the Dutch quarter of Smithfield, Roger gave vent to the fire of injustice that was burning in his bones.

"Why didn't you try to stop it, Henry?!" challenged Roger.

"Why didn't you just leave it alone when Dickens was only mouthin'?" argued Henry.

"Because Dickens was wrong! And so are you for bein' a coward about it. You know Jon is a Christian!" countered Roger.

"Course I am," said Jon, weakly, in his own defense.

"We all are, Roger," said Henry. "So don't think s' much about it! Sydrach says you think too much and. . ."

"Sydrach doesn't think at all!" snorted Roger. "And if we're all Christians, then I guess we shouldn't be beatin' each other up, should we?"

When they arrived at the Vanderhook home, Mrs. Vanderhook was much upset to see Jon in such shape. But as she listened to their story, she took time to look after Roger's arm, as well.

"God will bless you, Roger Williams, for your faithfulness to a friend," she said as she bandaged his elbow. "You have stuck closer than a brother to Jon today. I am proud of you, as your own mother and father should surely be. And thank you, too, Henry Adams, though you're old enough to have done a bit more than just bring home the wounded after the war!"

Henry Adams walked home that evening with his pride bruised and his conscience sorely challenged.

Roger Williams wandered back to Cow Lane with his heart aching but his head held high.

CHAPTER 3

1617–1621

"Who is that attentive young man back there?" asked Sir Edward Coke quietly to his wife.

Lady Hatton leaned toward her husband in the pew and whispered, "Which young man, Edward?"

"To our right, two rows back. The one so wrapped up in the sermon and taking notes so nicely in shorthand," said Sir Edward.

Lady Hatton turned discreetly and let her eyes wander through the Sunday morning congregation at St. Sepulchre's Church. Then she looked for the lad in question and promptly found him. Turning back, she faced the minister but quietly answered Sir Edward. "That's young Roger, son of James Williams. Williams is a merchant taylor here in Smithfield. His wife is the former Alice Pemberton. Her brother, James Pemberton, was our lord mayor of London a few years back."

"Ah, yes. Thank you, Dear," said Coke thoughtfully, as he turned his gaze toward the pulpit again. But his mind wandered from the message on God's kingdom to his own everpresent thoughts on the earthly kingdom and government of his native England.

Sir Edward Coke was chief justice of the King's Bench, the top judge in the land. At sixty-five years old, he was England's greatest and most famous legal expert. His clear eyes were used to noting details, and his keen mind was used to judging character. This Sabbath morning he was impressed with the apparent qualities of a young lad two pews back.

Roger was merely doing what was then required of all English schoolboys. Monday morning he would stand before the schoolmaster's desk to present a written outline on Sunday's sermon. He would be questioned about the biblical text that was preached, what it meant, and how it was to be applied to everyday life. Roger loved the Scriptures, and he took a serious delight in this bit of homework. Having learned at an early age how to write in shorthand, he used it often when taking notes or jotting down his thoughts. He was very good at it.

After the service, while Roger was greeting some friends, Sir Edward approached James Williams.

"Master Williams," said Sir Edward, "your son appears to be a pious young man with some talent in shorthand."

"Thank you, Sir Edward!" replied Roger's father, flattered by this unexpected appraisal of his boy. "His faith is a blessing to me and a reason for me to bless God. And his shorthand has served me well in my trade. It has served the Merchant Taylors' Company some, as well."

"Perhaps it could serve the king and the country at large. I would like to employ the young man," said Coke. "I would like him to take case notes for me at court—in the Star Chamber."

"Employ him?" said a startled Mr. Williams.

"How old is he?" asked Sir Edward.

"He's fourteen," answered Roger's father.

"He'll do fine," was the reply.

Roger could barely take notes the first day, sitting in that large courtroom with the glittering stars painted upon its

ROGER WILLIAMS

ceiling. In a long building behind Westminster Abbey in the
heart of London, the Star Chamber sat at the edge of Roger's
beloved Thames. Though he could walk home from there in
half an hour, it seemed that he was a world away from his
classroom in Smithfield. And indeed he was.

This was not the working-class world of his merchant-
dominated neighborhood; this was the world of politics and
power. This was not the taproom of St. George's Inn where
men's ideas and opinions flowed as freely as the beer; this
was the judgment seat of a nation where the rights and consciences of men were too often strangled by the unchallenged
power of the King's Court. This was not the docks in Smithfield where a lad could almost taste the freedoms that lay
beyond the salty blue horizon; this was the room in which
Bartholomew Legate had been sentenced to death for his religious beliefs.

Roger's awe of the lawyers dressed in scarlet faded as the
days turned into months. But his respect grew for the great
man who had hired him. And as the months turned into years,
Sir Edward grew to love this gentle and intelligent young son
of a merchant taylor. He loved him for his commitment to
God's truths, his passion for justice, and his heart for mercy.
He delighted in his insights on Scripture, his thoughts on the
court cases he was recording, and his opinions on the rights
of the individual. Coke, himself, though a powerful and popular man of great service to the king, had already been imprisoned twice for speaking out in behalf of the rights of the
common man.

One night the old lawyer and his young disciple sat

before a fire in Sir Edward's home. The judge's white beard seemed to glow in the firelight as he looked into Roger's bright face.

"What you say about freedom of religious conscience is quite true, Roger," said Sir Edward. "A man should be free before God to believe as his heart leads him. But if we all spoke our minds and demanded to live as we pleased, there would be chaos. God is not the author of chaos but of order. He is not the author of license but of law."

"But, Sir Edward, I am not saying we should live to please ourselves or to give in to the sin in our hearts. I am saying that we should be free under the law to worship God as we choose."

Roger rose from his chair and began to pace the room.

"Just last week," he continued, as the firelight threw his moving shadow upon the opposite wall, "the Chamber tortured, condemned, and threw an old man into prison for one heretical sentence that he wrote in a sermon that he never preached!"

"And if the court does not punish heresy, then how will the doctrines of the Lord remain pure?" challenged Sir Edward. "How can our nation remain free and be blessed by God if it allows His teachings to be twisted by every man's conscience?"

"Freedom does not come by the sword or the court," Roger replied. "Our Lord Jesus declared that only *He* can make a man free. So freedom comes by faith. And faith cannot be forced by either church or state, because true faith is a matter of the soul. It is between each man and God alone. So how can a nation be truly free or blessed by God if it does violence to the soul?"

"Would you have us put away our swords and be at the mercy of infidels, traitors, and rebels?" asked Sir Edward.

Roger shook his head emphatically. "No! The Scriptures say the sword is rightly raised against those who lie or steal or harm their neighbors, but neither the sword nor the bonfire should ever be used to persecute a man for ideas—even bad ideas."

"Your words are always stimulating, Master Roger, but I must change the subject radically before we say goodnight. Please be seated, will you?"

Roger sat down.

Sir Edward looked into the flames for a moment and then turned to Roger with a sincere and loving gaze. "Your faithful service to me these past four years, in the Star Chamber and in many an evening we've spent together, has been more than I can ever repay. You are like a son to me. And so I wish to do for you as I would for my own son. I want to send you on to preparatory school, that you might go on to Cambridge and to the ministry."

"I am honored, Sir Edward. Truly I am," Roger said. "But I have not served you for such privilege, and I am undeserving. . ."

"Nonsense, my boy! If anyone deserved the chance to serve God and the church in this way, it is you."

"But Father isn't well, Sir Edward, and I've been thinking he may need me by his side and in his shop."

"I have spoken with your father, Roger. His heart for you is even as I have just proposed. And the Church of England, as much as our Puritan brethren may not agree with all her traditions, needs young men of faith and fire like you."

Sir Edward rose from his chair and placed his hand on Roger's shoulder. "Your schooling will start at Charterhouse within a month."

CHAPTER 4

1621

At his father's bedside, Roger prayed. James Williams was dying. He had been feverish for a week and barely able to eat for half that time. Breathing became increasingly difficult as his weakened lungs strained painfully to pull air into his failing body. He could no longer sit up in bed. Today, he had hardly opened his eyes. Now the night was settling in.

"Father of mercies," Roger pleaded, "though heaven is more to be desired than all lands and riches on earth, still I would have my father here with me longer. Oh, God of grace and life, what a sad world this is!"

Roger opened his father's Bible upon the bed and turned the ragged pages until he came to the book of James. As his eyes passed slowly over the holy words, he stopped at a certain passage and read aloud. "Be afflicted, and mourn, and weep: let your laughter be turned to mourning, and your joy to heaviness."

His eyes swelled with hot tears, which he wiped upon the bedsheets. Then he read on, "For what is your life? It is even a vapour, that appeareth for a little time, and then vanisheth away."

Roger wept.

"Please, Roger, get some sleep," said a tender voice from the doorway. It was Catherine. She entered the room with a pan of water and began to gently wash her father's sweaty face with a cool, damp cloth.

"I can't leave him now, Catherine. I believe he may not see another morning. And then what shall we do? What is this life to be like without one who loved us so?"

Catherine ran her fingers through her brother's thick hair. "He loved us all, but he loved you most. It is your tenderness for Jesus that endeared you to him. Sydrach hates you for that, but perhaps the Lord will bring him to repentance."

Roger looked up into his sister's misty eyes. "Will Sydrach take care of Mother and Robert while I am at school?" he asked.

"Oh, yes," answered Catherine. "He can handle the shop as well as Father. My husband, Sam, will also give a hand when needed. But I fear we'll lose some business. Sydrach is too outspoken for the king. Father's Puritan friends may go elsewhere for their cloth. But we'll make out. Mother's relatives, the Pembertons, will help us if it comes to that."

"Sit with me," said Roger. "Pray with me for Father—for the family."

As the hours slowly moved toward a new dawn, Alice Williams quietly joined her two children in the watch. Elsewhere in the sad, silent house, Sydrach and Robert slept fitfully.

James Williams never awoke.

CHAPTER 5

1626

It was a late afternoon in May, and the students at Cambridge were on their daily liberty (a short period of free time before supper). In Roger's little room, three young men sat in heated conversation. A sharp-featured fellow named Jonas Lamb was loudly complaining about a recent hard turn of events.

"Seven years of our lives in preparation for the ministry! And now the high and mighty Charles the First declares by his 'sovereign power' that 'all further curious search into church doctrine be laid aside'! The Bible *commands* us to search the Scriptures! And I'd like to *know* what a man's to preach if not *true doctrine!*" Lamb said bitterly.

"Seven years is an awfully long time to be climbing the church stairs only to have the doors slammed in your face," said a stout little man named Richard Goddard.

"The keys to those doors are in Bishop Laud's hands," said Roger. "He'll just let us in *if* we promise to be obedient little Anglicans."

"Laud is worse than King Charles!" snorted Goddard.

"And Charles is worse than King James was!" added Lamb.

"But it's Laud who is stirring the king up against the Puritans," continued Goddard. "If the bishop weren't such a fanatic for the traditions of the Church of England, Puritan voices wouldn't be so severely silenced. All we want is to turn the Anglican Church more toward the church of the Bible!"

"We don't need some fancy parish church to preach in," said Roger with a wave of his arm. "We can declare the gospel in people's homes, in private meetings, in the streets if need be!"

The other men were silent for a moment. Then Goddard spoke again. "If we were to separate from the Church of England, then Laud would *really* be on our tails. How could we change things if we were religious outlaws? I think we must simply pray and hope that God changes the king's heart."

Roger got up and began to pace the room. "*Martin Luther* was a religious outlaw! Didn't God protect *him?* And didn't *he* change a few things?" he argued. "None of us in this room would ever have heard the gospel if he hadn't had the courage to stand up for the truth. If Laud wants someone to persecute, let's give him. . ."

There was a sharp knock at the door, and Roger opened it. It was the school's master, Jerome Beale. Behind him in the hallway were two armed soldiers.

"Good afternoon, Mr. Williams," greeted Beale. He looked around the room at the others seated there. "Best be readying yourselves for the evening meal, men," he said.

"What's going on here?" asked Lamb, as he got up from his stool and stared out the door at the soldiers.

"Mr. Williams is to travel with these men to see Bishop Laud," replied Master Beale. "I am assured that he will be treated as a gentleman and will return to us shortly."

Roger and his friends could hardly believe their ears.

"Sit here, please, Master Williams," said William Laud, pointing to a large chair next to his own.

Roger sat down and stared into the bishop's dark green eyes.

"I went to Cambridge, too," said Laud. "An excellent school."

"Yes, Sir, I am very grateful for my years within its walls," said Roger.

"As an alumnus, I have followed your academic progress," continued Laud, staring vacantly past Roger into the darkened corners of the spacious room. "Many of the students look up to you for your godly manner and your ability to argue your. . .your convictions and opinions. Of course, your sponsor, Sir Edward Coke, has set you an excellent example in these things."

Roger sat up in his chair, a proud gleam in his eyes. "A man of honor, wisdom, and piety; indeed, a glorious light! Since my own father died, Sir Edward has often called me his son. Truly, his instruction and encouragement have spurred me on in all that I do!"

"Of course, of course," said Laud, looking Roger in the face. "And Coke is a man who is not afraid to question tradition or authority when he sees a falsehood in it. Even if it means opposing the king."

"For this I love him most!" Roger said.

"For opposing the king?" asked Laud.

"For opposing falsehood," said Roger.

"But let's speak of Cambridge again," continued the bishop. "Our college years seem to be a time when we're inclined to question the truths and traditions that we. . ."

"Bishop Laud," interrupted Roger, "I have spent most of my life questioning traditions and searching for truth in the

Scriptures. I believe it is the duty of every Christian to do so."

The bishop stared at Roger grimly.

"May we get to the point for which you summoned me?" asked Roger.

"I will present the questions, Mr. Williams," said Laud.

Roger was silent.

"How do you spend your free time at the university, Mr. Williams?"

"Generally, in biblical studies and discussion," answered Roger.

"Have you been to a Separatist meeting?" queried Laud.

"Many times," said Roger. "Since I was a boy. Have you never been to one, Sir?"

The bishop ignored the question. "You've been taking your free-time biblical studies in Smithfield, haven't you? At the underground meetings of the Separatist Puritan leader Derek Baxter, haven't you? And you've even been *preaching* at some of those gatherings, haven't you?"

Roger said nothing.

"And you have spoken out against the king and his church!" challenged Laud.

At this, Roger could not be silent. "The church is *Christ's,* not the *king's.* Not the bishops' nor the elders'. Not yours nor mine," he replied.

Laud grew red in the face, and he blew air from his puffed cheeks. "You have denied the king's right to punish those who disagree with the Church of England!" challenged Laud.

"Weren't all Protestants, men just like you and me, judged 'heretics' when Bloody Mary was our queen?" Roger argued. "When she burned those who disagreed with *her,* was it her divine right to do so? Was it within her sovereign power? Or did she do so out of her own human opinions and prejudices?"

Laud stood up. A big man even when seated, he seemed larger than himself when he was angry. He was getting very angry.

"*Mary* was the heretic, as you well know, Williams! She was a pawn of Satan and the antichrist! But Charles is the true king, a true Christian! The Anglican Church is the true church! And I am a true bishop under God," Laud steamed.

"I am ordering you in the name of the king to cease your preaching against the crown! If you continue, you will stand at court on charges of treason!" continued Bishop Laud, standing over Roger and shaking a stiff finger in his face. "And as for your graduate ministerial studies at Cambridge, you might as well quit because you can forget about *ever* having a pulpit of your own!"

Now Roger was standing. The two men were face-to-face. Laud's fists were clenched. His body was tensed.

Roger opened his mouth to speak, but he stopped himself. Swallowing heavily and fighting back angry tears, he lowered his eyes to the floor. *Lord God, help me to hold my tongue!* he prayed within himself.

Laud slowly relaxed and then stepped back. For a long moment, no one spoke. Then the bishop quietly and coldly said, "You may go now."

It was dark when Roger left the bishop's house. As he started off on foot toward Cambridge, he became aware that he was being followed. Glancing back over his shoulder, he could see a man about his height, close behind but always in the shadows. Turning a corner near a noisy brew house, Roger sank back into the cover of some dark bushes. Shortly, the man came around the corner, too. Stopping suddenly, he looked up and down the dimly lit street.

"Roger?" said the man, quietly at first, with his back to the bushes. Roger thought his voice was familiar, but. . .

"Roger Williams?" said the man again, more loudly this time, as he turned in yet another direction. And then, from the light that shone from the brew house windows, Roger recognized his pursuer.

"Jon!" exclaimed Roger, stepping out from his hiding place.

"Whoa!" shouted Jon Vanderhook, stumbling backwards in surprise. "Roger! You *scared* me!" he said.

"As you scared *me,* you thief in the night! What are you doing coming after me like this?"

"We heard that Laud had sent for you, so I came to watch for you and to bring a message from your Separatist Puritan friends."

"Come! Walk with me, and tell me about it," said Roger. "I do hope it's good news after the trials of this evening! I've been accused of preaching against the king, Jon. And as long as Laud is bishop, he will keep me from any pulpit with the Church of England."

Roger threw his eyes toward the starry heavens and shouted into the night sky, *"Let* the king be king, I say, and God bless him! But let the church be the church! There is room only for *one king* on the spiritual throne of thrones: *Jesus!"*

"Perhaps I do have good news for you," said Jon. "You may have your pulpit sooner than you think."

"Tell me, Jon!"

"Sir William Masham wants you for his chaplain."

"Chaplain of Otes Estate? 'Tis far better than a parish in London, Jon! And no bishop can forbid it. Praise the Almighty; I'll take it."

CHAPTER 6

1629–1630

Otes Manor, in Essex County, was about ten miles outside London. Like many country estates of the time, it was a self-sufficient community. Within Masham's grounds, wheat was grown to provide bread for the household. Sheep were raised, and flax was planted for the weaving, dyeing, cutting, and fashioning of clothing. Candles were crafted from peeled rushes dipped in tallow. There were barns and granaries, orchards and fields, animals and laborers. Within the Masham manor houses, there was a washroom, a folding chamber, a brew house, a malt house, a dairy, a cheese loft, a buttery, a dry larder, and a pastry house. There were bedrooms, kitchens, baths, dining rooms, sitting rooms, a library, and a chapel.

A chaplain of such an estate, as Roger now was, was actually pastor of a private parish. His duty was to look after the souls of the entire household, from master to mistress to the servants who watered the sheep and fed the pigs.

Sir William Masham was a Puritan and a member of Parliament. Jailed once for opposing a war tax decreed by the king, he was an outspoken voice for reform in both the church and the government of England. His massive estate at Otes was a secret meeting place for many of the most powerful Puritans in Parliament.

But Parliament was a little *too* powerful for King Charles. It often disagreed with his decrees and too often passed laws in favor of the rights of the commoner. So, in March of 1629, Charles put an end to Parliament. Roger was there with Masham in London when Parliament's old wooden doors were closed and locked by order of the king.

"What is happening to our nation?" asked Sir William, as he and Roger rode home on horseback down the rutted highway toward Essex. "When a king takes the laws of the land into his own hands, who can be free from his long arm?"

"What is happening to the church?" added Roger. "When a bishop declares what prayers can be prayed and what prayers cannot, who can be free to worship God?"

"Roger, the church is ever on your mind! But the church itself is not free in England. She is under the thumb of non-Christian clergy and full of unrepentant sinners. I wonder lately if she can ever be free," said Sir William.

Sir William suddenly spurred his horse on faster. "Follow me!" he called to Roger. Roger kicked his mare to catch up.

Sir William rode faster still as the two men and their horses galloped neck and neck over the dusty road.

"It's a race we're in!" shouted Masham over the noise of the pounding hooves. "We must stay ahead of the king and his bishop. We must preach the gospel while it is day, and ride long into the night if need be."

"But if we are always running, who will build or plant? There can be no fruits of righteousness if no one plants an orchard," replied Roger.

" 'Tis truth you speak, Roger! Indeed, some must plant. But others must run!" shouted Sir William.

"And while we run from the king, where shall we run to?" asked Roger, ducking under a low-hanging branch as the horses thundered down the familiar land.

"I did not say we should run *from* the king, only that we must stay *ahead* of him," yelled Sir William as the gates of Otes came into view. "But in so doing, perhaps we shall run to the sea. Perhaps we shall sail beyond the horizon. Perhaps we shall plant God's vineyard and build Christ's church in a land *beyond* the reach of England's corrupted crown!"

" 'Your old men shall dream dreams,' " quoted Roger.

" 'Your young men shall see visions,' " returned Sir William. "You must *capture* this vision, young man!"

"You've been talking to Winthrop again, haven't you?" laughed Roger, reining his sweaty horse in front of the house.

The late July sun was still high over Sempringham Castle when the mud-encrusted figure of John Winthrop rode wearily up to its doors. The servant who let him in was surprised at his soiled appearance and hurried to bring him water and a change of clothes. Winthrop gratefully washed his hands and face but refused the clothes. He was anxious to begin the business for which he had ridden so far.

The servant led him down a long hall toward a massive pair of intricately carved doors.

Behind those doors sat a prestigious gathering of Puritan gentlemen: ministers and lords, businessmen and politicians. Roger was there, having come by horseback with two other ministers: John Cotton and Thomas Hooker.

As Winthrop entered the room, his disheveled appearance caused many to rise in alarm.

"What on earth happened to you, Winthrop?" exclaimed Sir Richard Saltonstall, the lord of Ledsham Manor.

"The same that has happened to all men on earth. I have fallen, Sir Richard," replied the forty-three-year-old ex-lawyer, brushing his damp curly hair from his narrow, bearded face. "In a bog near Ely on my way. 'Tis the Lord's way of reminding me that only by His grace can I stand clean before Him."

"And 'tis a lesson to the rest of us not to judge a man by his appearance!" laughed Sir Richard.

The humorous exchange put the gathering at ease. Winthrop greeted each man present and then settled himself into a vacant chair at the head of the long oak table.

"And now, Mr. Hooker," he said, "would you ask the Lord to lead us in our time here together?"

Hooker prayed, "Father of mercies, great and mighty, we beg Thee this day to be among us by Thy Spirit and to guide Thy poor servants in this vast undertaking.

"We are utterly lost without Thee, and we ask Thee to go before us as Thou went before the Israelites in the wilderness. Show us Thy cloud by day that we may follow Thee and Thy fire by night that we may see Thy presence and know Thy nearness.

"Lead us into Thy Promised Land that we may live by Thy laws only. That we may glorify Thy name and the name of Thy Holy Son, Jesus, among the heathen and to all the nations.

"In all our ways, we acknowledge Thee. In all our plans, we trust Thee. Make our paths straight to that New Jerusalem beyond the seas!"

Long into the candlelit night they conferred. With Bibles opened and maps spread out before them, they talked of ships and money, of politics and law, of homes and family. And when all was done, a historic decision had been made:

They would buy up the Massachusetts Bay Company—take it over completely—in order to fill Massachusetts with Puritans. They would then begin to build a biblical society, under Winthrop's leadership, in the New World.

The Massachusetts Bay Company was an English colonial enterprise already operating in New England. It had founded Boston and Salem and a few other small villages in the Massachusetts Bay area. If the Sempringham group could buy the company, they could help other Puritans to move their families across the sea and build a new order based upon the laws and principles of God's Word. Though they didn't plan to separate from the fellowship of the Anglican Church, they would still be separated from Old England by the great Atlantic. This would set them free from the persecution of King Charles and Bishop Laud. They could worship God in freedom at last.

As the meeting came to an end, Winthrop's warm, piercing eyes looked around the room at the gathering of tired but excited men. His gaze came to rest upon a large wall tapestry of an old map of England.

"Our nation is heading for disaster," he said with sorrow. "Laud has been transferred to London, where he has begun to shut down Puritan pulpits. He is fast putting out the holy light of the true gospel."

The candles had burnt low upon the huge table, and Winthrop took one from its holder. He lifted it above his head so that its flame threw a flickering light into the rafters of the high ceiling.

"It may please God to use *us,* in *New* England, to light such a candle that will shine back here from across the sea," he said. "Let us commit ourselves to that purpose, to show our countrymen the way to a more glorious life in God's presence and service. This we shall do in His care and for His name's sake."

In the spring of 1630, eleven ships, filled with Puritan families, household servants, livestock, and provisions, set sail from Old England toward a new life and a new society over the seas.

Aboard the flagship *Arbella*—a 350-ton, 38-cannon vessel —John Winthrop delivered a speech that he called "A Model of Christian Charity." He reminded everyone of their calling to this new life together, of the holy society they would be building, of the love and commitment they must have for one another, and of his determination to succeed.

But Roger Williams was not yet a part of this "Great Migration." Back at the Masham estate, he had fallen in love. In December of 1629, he and Mary Barnard had been married in the parish church at High Laver, near Otes.

As the Massachusetts-bound ships sailed slowly from the shores of Old England, Roger and Mary Williams bade them good-bye. Though Roger's heart was with them, he was not fully at peace about the venture.

"I love those men, Mary," he said one night as the newly-weds sat near the fire in their room at Otes. "Winthrop, especially. Though I don't know him well, I believe he is a great man. His vision is a great vision. And I long to be with him in the wilderness. I long especially to share in the preaching of the gospel among the natives, for I greatly desire their souls for God. But. . ." And he sighed deeply as he stirred the hot coals with an iron poker.

"But what, my dear?" asked Mary, leaning her head upon his shoulder with her arms around his waist.

"But, what is the sense of crossing the sea and yet remaining part of the Church of England? How can God bless a mission that is tainted by the blood of a church that wears an earthly crown, persecutes Christians, and forces the unconverted to sit in its pews?" he replied.

"Perhaps Mr. Winthrop will renounce the Anglican Church once he is settled in Massachusetts," offered Mary.

"Perhaps," agreed Roger thoughtfully. "He is wise. He is godly. He surely isn't lacking in courage. Perhaps, after passing over the waves and taking up his role as governor of the colony. . .perhaps."

In December of 1630, Roger traveled to London to visit his aging mother. While he was there, Sydrach pestered him about his Separatist views.

"Separation from the Anglican Church is disobedience to the king," argued Sydrach. "And since the king is God's anointed, given by heaven to rule our nation, then disobedience to the king is treason against God!"

But Roger was tired of debate with his bitter older brother. "Can't you just let me be what God has made me to be?" Roger pleaded.

"God has nothing to do with what you've become," sneered Sydrach. "You're just a troublemaker and a spiritual snob! And you'll surely get what's coming to you someday."

Roger turned from Sydrach to his mother. "I'll be going now, Mother," he said, as he kissed her on the forehead. "You are all in my prayers." With a last pained glance at Sydrach, he headed out the door.

But Sydrach followed him at a distance and watched as he stopped in to visit his Separatist friends in the home of Derek Baxter.

"The bishop gave you a warning once, little brother," said Sydrach to the shadows that surrounded him. "I helped you to his attention then, and I believe I'll pay you the honor once again!"

Sydrach, like a Judas, hurried away toward the home of the "High Priest." Laud would be happy to see him.

No sooner had Roger returned to Otes than a messenger from London arrived, summoning him to appear before the bishop on the following day.

"I won't go," Roger told Mary. "If he wants my company so badly, let him come *here* to have tea with me!"

"But you will bring trouble down upon the whole house of Masham," pleaded Mary. "God direct us; what shall we do?"

Roger stared out into the cold November night.

"We must stay ahead of the king and his bishop," said Roger. "Perhaps we shall sail beyond the horizon." He turned to Mary. She ran to his arms and buried her face in his cloak.

Roger continued, "Captain Pierce is back from Massachusetts with his ship, the *Lyon*. He has spent several weeks readying cargo of supplies to take back to New England. He leaves in two days."

"Do we sail with him, Roger?" asked Mary, looking up into her husband's troubled eyes.

"I believe we must," he replied.

CHAPTER 7

1631–1636

"Susannah, look!" exclaimed Molly Winters, dropping her basket of mussels on the beach. She pointed toward the wide horizon where the dark blue waters of Massachusetts Bay met the grey-clouded February sky.

"A ship!" both women shouted, as they gathered up their skirts and ran across the rocks toward the village of Nantasket.

The *Lyon,* with its cargo of twenty passengers and two hundred tons of food, had safely made its way across the storm-tossed ocean. Those aboard were gratefully rejoicing at the sight of land, for they had not felt it beneath their feet in fifty-seven days. Those on land were gratefully rejoicing at the sight of their deliverance, for the colony's food supply was almost gone. A recent proclamation declaring February 6 as a day of humbled fasting was exchanged for a day of thankful feasting. God had answered the colony's prayers twenty-four hours before they were uttered!

Roger and Mary were welcomed to the New World and given a room in the house of Governor Winthrop in Boston. As the weeks passed, the Williamses became familiar with this "New Jerusalem," and Roger was a guest preacher on Sunday afternoons in the thatched meetinghouse at the head of Boston's only street. To a man who'd been London-born and raised, this rugged little village between the cold sea and the wooded wilderness hardly seemed like either Eden or

Jerusalem. But Roger wasn't concerned about either comfort or culture. His heart burned with a passion for biblical Christianity and a purified church, concerns that overshadowed his present primitive surroundings.

In March, John Wilson, pastor of the Boston Church, announced that he was returning to England to fetch his wife back to Massachusetts. Wilson suggested to the governor and the colony's ruling magistrates that Roger Williams take his place in the pulpit during his absence. The magistrates unanimously agreed, and they formally offered Roger the honored post.

But Roger turned them down. Boston was astounded.

"What is your reason for refusing this pulpit, Master Williams?" asked Winthrop as he and Roger sat together in Winthrop's study.

"I dare not give communion to an unseparated people," Roger bluntly said. "As long as Boston still holds the hand of the English church, she touches the robes of antichrist."

"Antichrist! Williams, the Anglican Church may be less than pure, but she is Protestant! And there are many godly men and women within her fellowship," countered Winthrop.

"The Anglican Church is a false church," argued Roger. "Her roots don't reach to the apostles. They are tangled in the rocky soil of the Roman Catholic apostasy, and they suck their poisoned doctrines from the council chambers of the king.

"We must 'come out from among them,' as the apostle Paul commands us," Roger insisted. "We must repent and separate ourselves from the English church completely, if we are ever to recover the lost Zion."

"Did your ocean journey upset your senses as well as your stomach, Williams? This colony *depends* on our company charter from the king. If we loose ourselves from the Anglican Church, we risk the loss of our right to exist! Should we tempt the Lord by cutting off the branch while we sit on it? Though I mourn the corruption of our mother church, still I believe she has the nature of the truth in her," reasoned Winthrop.

But Roger could not be convinced, and at last he bid the governor good-night.

Winthrop sat alone in his darkened study, puzzled by this godly young zealot who had begun to trouble the waters of the Massachusetts Bay Colony.

Weeks turned into months, and the men of Boston—Williams and Winthrop included—rolled up their sleeves in the common work of thicket-clearing, wall-raising, wood-gathering, and fence-building. Hay was gathered on nearby islands. Framed, thatched cottages began to replace the many wigwams and tents of the Puritan planters. But before spring arrived or anyone had yet prepared a garden or a crop, Roger was sowing more seeds of discontent. In his commitment to proclaim the truth as he saw it, he didn't seem to realize that he was tugging at the rug upon which his friends and neighbors stood.

This time he challenged the magistrates' right to punish Sabbath-breaking.

The magistrates were the colony's lawmakers and policemen. Committed to the Puritan vision of a community built upon biblical laws and morality, they firmly believed that God would bless them and dwell among them only as the community sought to obey Him. In the Massachusetts Bay Colony, the Puritans were Congregationalists. That meant that members of each church congregation chose their own pastors and ran their own affairs. They also elected the magistrates and the governor that would oversee the business of colonial government. This was very different from the English church where all congregations were ruled by ministers appointed by the bishop, and the bishop himself was appointed by the king. However, though the Bay churches were glad their English king was far across the waters, they still believed that government must enforce the laws of both the state and the church.

The foundational laws of the Bay were the Ten Commandments that God had given Moses. There were no higher laws known to man, so upon these commandments the magistrates laid the stones of their New Jerusalem.

To insure that the people lived, and hopefully believed, according to God's principles, everyone was required to go to church on Sundays (once in the morning and once in the afternoon) and on certain other days of the week. The commandment to "honor the Sabbath and keep it holy" was strictly enforced, and no one was allowed to work or travel (except to church) on Sunday. Those who "broke the Sabbath" were sometimes fined, sometimes publicly admonished, whipped, or placed in the stocks. The nature of their Sabbath-breaking determined the type of punishment. The law for Sunday church attendance was also a law in England at the time, and most folks didn't think it a strange requirement for life in the land that acknowledged God and His Son, Jesus Christ.

But not all folks think alike.

"The apostle Paul tells us that each man may keep his own Sabbath. It is a matter of conscience between an individual and

God," Roger reasoned. "And if a man is not a Christian, how can we force him to honor the Sabbath at all?"

The magistrates disagreed. "If we allow everyone to do as he pleases, our colony will fall apart at the seams. We have covenanted to submit ourselves to God and to our leaders," they said. "We cannot build a holy society if we let unholiness and disorder run loose in the streets."

Roger believed there must be punishment for those who broke God's laws in regard to relationships and property, but he argued that the laws of the First Table (the first four of the Ten Commandments) were matters between each person and God alone. Roger's contentions were threatening the authority of the men responsible for peace and order in the colony. Couldn't he see that he was digging a pit for them all to fall into?

But Roger couldn't see it, and so he kept on digging. Meanwhile, the magistrates could not agree on what to do about the man. Apart from his strange opinions, they respected and admired him. He was a good and honest neighbor, a gifted preacher, and an unselfish, compassionate, and hard-working member of the community. Perhaps he would see the errors of his way.

In April of that year, the nearby town of Salem invited Roger to assist their ailing pastor, Samuel Skeleton, and to be teacher in the place of their former pastor, John Higginson (who had died the preceding summer). Believing Salem to be more Separatist at heart, Roger accepted. But Winthrop was worried that this young firebrand would cause too much trouble if given a pulpit from which to spread his weird philosophies. The assistants (the Governor's Council) strongly advised the Salem congregation to think twice before installing Roger Williams as their new pastor, but Salem had already made its decision.

Roger and Mary moved to Salem, and Roger assumed the pulpit. But his rigidly Separatist views proved too strong for Salem as well, and it wasn't long before the Williamses chose to pack up their belongings again. This time they sailed twenty-five miles south, out of Puritan jurisdiction and into strictly Separatist territory. Their destination: Plymouth.

Roger became a Pilgrim.

The hillside settlement of Plymouth had been born out of a Separatist congregation that had moved from England to Holland in 1608 to escape persecution. In 1620, it pulled up roots again, sailing for the New World in a small ship called the *Mayflower*. The Plymouth colony was older and larger than either Boston or Salem. It was more prosperous as well, and allowed its citizens a bit more freedom, but it was beginning to wane in its spiritual fervor and mission. Roger sensed the spiritual laxity and rose to the occasion, assisting Pastor Ralph Smith in the care of the souls of Plymouth.

Meanwhile, Roger hoed his acre of land and planted his corn. He purchased cattle from Boston through Winthrop. He learned the Dutch language from his neighbors who had lived in Holland.

He made many new friends. There was the cheerful patriarch and elder, William Brewster, with his library of four hundred books. There was the prudent and godly governor, William Bradford, who had recently turned—in his spare time—to the study of Hebrew and to the writing of poetry and a *History of Plymouth Plantation.* There was the fiery little soldier and guardian of Plymouth, Captain Miles Standish. There was the softhearted Pilgrim deacon, psalm-singer, and physician, Samuel Fuller. There was the ex-printer, merchant, and Indian expert, Edward Winslow. It was Winslow who led Roger into the woods one day to meet a man who would change Roger's life.

The sunlight filtered through the tall oaks, highlighting patches of gold and green upon the thickly ferned forest floor. Birds flew and deer fled as Edward and Roger slid past moss-covered rocks and over the giant rotted skeleton of an ancient spruce. The path they were following was a slim, well-worn trail that wound through the tall trees toward a village of the Narragansett Indians.

As they came out of the woods into a clearing beside a flowing stream, they spotted a dark-skinned native washing his hands and face at the edge of the water.

"What cheer, *Nétop* (friend)?" Edward shouted to the man.

"Asco wequassunnúmmis (good morning), *Nétop!"* returned the tall, thin Indian. "What brings you to our country, Winslow?"

"I am here to see Canonicus, Wassáppi," replied Edward. "He is expecting us. I have brought a friend who wishes to meet him."

Wassáppi guided the two Englishmen into the village and to the door of the house of the Grand Sachem, Canonicus. The sachem's dwelling was a long building of poles, covered over with mats made of animal hides. It had three fires inside and three fire holes in its ceiling. Its inside walls were decorated with colorfully embroidered mats made by the women of the village.

"Come in, Winslow," said the aged sachem. "Come in and sit down."

Edward and Roger entered the smokey dwelling, and for a moment Roger could hardly breathe.

Canonicus remained seated and motioned for them to recline. When they had done so, the great chief spread his arms out to them in greeting and smiled.

Prince over the nation of the Narragansetts—by far the largest and most powerful tribe in New England—Canonicus had ruled for many decades. Though seventy years of age, the sachem still had his health and his wits. The English feared him for the authority he held, but they respected him for his wisdom and his genuine desire to live at peace with them. He, in his turn, respected the English for their superior inventions, their powerful weapons, and their great ships. He was wise enough to see that the ships kept coming. *Perhaps,* he thought, *they will always come. If so, I must lead my people to stand firmly on our land but always at peace when peace is offered.* Though he was puzzled that *Manìt* (the Narragansett god) had allowed the English to come into his land, he was not afraid of what each day held. But he felt that the God of the English must be more powerful than the god of the Indians, because He had given the English books and clothes and many other marvelous things.

In fact, God was the subject of this day's conversation and the reason for Roger's first visit to the house of Canonicus.

"I am Canonicus," said the old sachem to the young Pilgrim. "You are Roger Williams. You wish to talk about God.

We will talk about God."

And for the next three hours, the Indian king and the English preacher talked religion. In that short time, on that sunny summer morning, their two hearts were strangely united in a bond of affection and respect that would grow stronger and truer in the years ahead. As the time came for Roger and Edward to depart, Canonicus made one last comment concerning their discussion:

"You have shown me the Book which God Himself made, concerning men's souls. I cannot read its writings as you can. So perhaps you know more than I do about these things. Still, I must trust my forefathers, for they received their knowledge from god, as well."

"There is one God and one truth," replied Roger, "just as there is one Canonicus. If another of your people should claim to be Canonicus and should declare things in your name, yet he is not Canonicus, and his words are not yours, whoever follows him would be following a false sachem."

Canonicus nodded thoughtfully. "We will talk more of these matters on another day," he said.

As the seasons came and went, Roger spent more and more time among the Indians. With Winslow's help, he set up a trading business with them and contacted his brother Robert in England to arrange for shipments of goods to Plymouth. He learned the Narrangansett language and customs and preached to them at all opportunities. He met sachems of other tribes. He slept in their smokey tents. He ate with them around their fires. And as his heart was more and more inclined toward their souls, he wrote to Winthrop that he would like to be a missionary among them. During this time of concourse with the natives, he formed some ideas that would get him into more trouble than he had yet known in this new world.

"Mary, I'm beginning to believe that the land upon which the English stand is sinfully won," said Roger one evening as he warmed his feet by the fire of his hearth.

Mary urged him on with a surprised nod as she stirred the soup that hung over the flames.

Roger continued, "This land was the natives' before we came. Before the English or the Dutch or the French. The Indians settled it and farmed it and hunted it for generations that only God knows of. And yet with one planting of the English flag on its soil, the king declares it his. Then he gives it to whomever he wills but with no consideration of its native population."

"Roger, it belongs to England by right of discovery, and we have it from the king's hand as a gift from God," replied Mary, puzzled by her husband's latest revelations.

"Discovery? It was already discovered, and indeed inhabited, by the savages who have lived upon it for years. And they consider it a gift from God as well, though they know Him not," said Roger. "I have thought about this much and have been writing about it whenever I have a moment to spare. I mean to share my thoughts with Governor Bradford if ever I find the time."

"God will make the time when He has set the purpose, dear Roger," said Mary with resignation. "But, here, the soup is ready."

After a prayer of thanksgiving and blessing for God's provision, Roger and Mary quietly ate their supper. Mary kept her eyes on the man she loved as he sat in silent thought. She waited for him to come out of his dreaming in order to tell him something that had been upon her heart all day. But he seemed to be so far away this night, and he didn't speak again until the meal had ended.

"Thank you," he said suddenly, looking up at Mary with a warm smile. "The soup was delicious. I am full and satisfied."

Mary pulled her chair closer to his and reached out to hold his calloused hands.

"Roger," she said, with a gentle glimmer in her eyes.

"Yes, Dearest," he replied, returning her gaze with a tired but attentive sigh.

"Roger," she began again, "you are going to be a father."

In June of 1633, only two months before Mary was due to have her baby, Roger received a message from Salem. Samuel Skeleton, like his predecessor at Salem, was slowly dying of tuberculosis. Though Salem had chafed at the preaching of Williams only two years earlier, it was in desperate need of someone to assume the burden of five services a week. Knowing Roger was a committed and gifted teacher, the congregation called upon him once again.

Out of pity for his dying friend, and believing it to be a temporary change, Roger returned to Salem. He was thirty years old.

In August, little Mary Williams was born. But with the joys of parenthood came the responsibilities of the same. As Skeleton grew less able to lead, Roger was soon saddled with the main care of the Salem church. Added to Roger's load was his continued trade and preaching among the Indians, along with the farming of his land. His days were hard and long, and they left Roger wearied and weakened.

Still, he pressed on, and under his preaching, the Salem congregation experienced a deep conviction of sin and a revived spiritual life in God. Under the influence of Roger's zeal and eloquence, moved by his warmheartedness and his sterling character, Salem took on the image of its new spiritual leader. Much to the dismay of the rest of the colony, the town became a stronghold of radical Separatism.

On top of it all, while still in Plymouth, Roger had managed to finish his little treatise on land rights. Winthrop had recently heard of it through Bradford, and he was much disturbed. He asked Roger for a copy, and when he had read it, he shared it with his assistants. After digesting the unsettling contents of the pamphlet, which basically disputed the right of Massachusetts and New Plymouth to their land, the assistants summoned Roger.

In Boston, in March of 1634, Roger stood before the governor and his court.

"Master Williams," said Winthrop, "if God wasn't pleased in giving us this land, why did He drive out the natives before us? Why does He still make room for us by sending the smallpox among the savages, diminishing them that we may increase? Why has He planted His churches here?"

"Sir," replied Roger humbly, "I must admit that God has slain many of the natives by His own hand and that we are here in their stead, but it is beyond my understanding."

Winthrop continued, "Even if we had no right to this land, God has full right to it. If He is pleased to give it to us, taking it from a people who have so long usurped Him, who shall argue with Him?"

"I shall not," replied Roger. "But neither shall I claim the land as mine unless I pay for it out of my own pocketbook. The king, though he calls this land his own, has no more right to give it away than Canonicus has the right to give London away to the Narragansetts."

"How can you say this?" asked Winthrop. "I agree with you that as a colony we must deal as Christians with the savages. But the right of discovery is international law! And to speak against the king will only provoke him against us. If you truly loved the peace of our churches in New England, you would not so rashly put a sword in the king's hand to destroy us!"

Roger felt the sting, and indeed the truth, of Winthrop's words. Though he fully believed the logic of his own arguments, he could not deny the logic of the court. Looking around at the judicial gathering, he apologized for the anguish and concern his book had caused them.

"I meant it only to be a sharing of my private thoughts with Governor Bradford," Roger explained. "I am sorry it has drug us all to court and to controversy. You may burn it, or any part of it, for all I care."

But Roger did not remain penitent for long. His love for the natives, his hatred for the "anti-Christian" Church of England, and his passion for truth as he saw it, overpowered the sensible reasonings of Governor Winthrop. He resumed his preaching against the king's right to give away land in New England, and he condemned the sinfulness of those who accepted it from the king. He even wrote a letter to Charles, accusing him of various sins against God and admonishing him to repent.

Meanwhile, news had arrived from England that Charles was planning to revoke the Bay Company's charter and to appoint a royal governor in New England. And Laud, with the king's permission, was threatening to impose Anglican discipline upon the colony. In fact, a ship had been built especially to carry the new governor to the New World.

But God, with His eye out for the redeemed of New England (and for reasons that were surely His alone), headed the king off at the pass. While the new ship was being launched, it split in half and sank.

Divine intervention or not, Roger could not have picked a worse time to be railing against the king or the Anglican Church. But truth was truth to him. Let the heads fall where they may!

The final straw in his attack on Bay authority came in his opposition to their *Oath of Fidelity* and their request for a standard church discipline for all the Bay congregations.

Roger spoke out against this unified church discipline and against the magistrates' right to enforce it, because he felt that it struck at the heart of an independent congregation's right to run its own race under God. The magistrates understood his logic, but they were getting tired of his repeated attacks against their authority. Didn't he know that these were dangerous times and that a stronger hand was needed at the helm of the government? They didn't want to take away freedoms; they wanted to insure them for the future by pulling things together during this time of crisis.

The *Oath* was an attempt by the magistrates to insure the loyalty of Bay residents against the threat of Charles and his royal governor. Since many strangers had recently arrived in the Bay with no intent to settle in the colony, the magistrates needed a way to make them promise to abide by the laws of the land while they were living there. Surely Roger could see the need for that.

But Roger's eyes were clouded. Perhaps it was the incredible daily load he labored under. Perhaps it was the tearing away from one civilized, all-familiar world to the wild, blank slate of another. Perhaps it was the sickness that he now endured, that kept him under the care of two physicians (but rarely kept him from his duties). Perhaps it was the constant tension between him and the Bay, a tension strained to the breaking point by continual callings before the Court of Assistants. Perhaps it was simply the pride and passion of a youthful idealism that carried his biblical conscience above the practical realities of maintaining a stable government in the wilderness. Whatever it was that drove Roger to declare his personal position at all points, he spoke out against the *Oath* with apparently no recognition of the problem the magistrates were trying to meet. His words, too often, gave others reason to rebel against the government.

His own reason, as always, was not political but spiritual.

"We must never ask an unsaved man to take an oath before God. An oath is something between a man's conscience and the Almighty," argued Roger. "Besides, the Lord Jesus said that no man should swear an oath. We are to say 'Yes' or 'No' to all that is asked of us. Anything else, Scripture declares, is from the evil one."

The magistrates, the Bay ministers, the governor and his assistants—indeed most anyone in the Bay—would gladly have entered a discussion on the words of Jesus. They did so each Sunday in order to better understand the commands and the ways of God. They did so as they went about their days fishing, hunting, farming, building, trading, eating, drinking, and playing. But this cyclone from Salem was blowing up a storm that far exceeded the gentle winds of doctrinal debate. This storm must be stilled, or the authority of the magistrates would be brought to nothing; and the Bay would be thrown into civil dissension. A house divided cannot stand.

"Was Williams this much of a radical back in Old England?" asked newly elected Governor John Haynes to a special gathering of Bay ministers on chilly a October day in 1635.

Haynes had arrived in New England, along with Roger's old friends John Cotton and Thomas Hooker, in September of 1633. Hooker became pastor at Newtown, and Cotton accepted the Boston pulpit which Roger had refused. Haynes had beat out Winthrop in a recent election for the governorship.

"Perhaps he was and simply didn't declare it as loudly or as often," answered Cotton. "But in coming here he has discovered himself."

Haynes did not know Roger as Winthrop did. He had no special affection for him or appreciation for his better qualities. He only saw Williams as a troublemaker whose trouble must be ended, one way or another, immediately.

On October 8, Roger—though sick—came once more to court. It was no ordinary assembly that was gathered at the Newtown Church for the general court session. Besides all the ministers in the Bay, the magistrates and the assistants were also present. Governor Haynes presided.

"Master Williams," said Hooker, who had been chosen to

convince Roger of the error of his actions and opinions. "Will you not cease in your digging of ditches beneath our churches? Will you not hear the arguments of your brothers and colleagues? Will you not bow before God in the matter of obedience to the civil authorities of the Bay?"

"I bow before God daily, Thomas," answered Roger. "My life and breath, what there is of both, are His alone. My allegiance is His alone."

"What of Paul's words to the Romans that whoever resists the power of the civil authorities is therefore resisting the ordinances of God?" questioned Hooker.

Roger was stunned. How often had he heard that argument from the lips of English kings and bishops? Heard it used to shame good church folk into mindless submission. How often had they all heard it? And hadn't they crossed the seas—Hooker included—to escape the persecution of men who claimed a special right to divine authority? Roger simply shook his fever-flushed face in disbelief and posed a question of his own.

"Do not the civil authorities of the Bay, whom I respect for men of godliness and faithfulness, also need to bow before God? My arguments against them are not against their authority, but against an un-Christian use of it."

Hooker quickly retorted, "Then you hold to all that you have spoken against them? To all that you have written? To all that you have done to tear down what they would build?"

Roger's reddened eyes flashed with conviction and pain. Not conviction of any sin of his own, unfortunately, but of the rightness of his opinions. Not with pain for the men who had patiently endured his attacks but for their misunderstanding his heart. Pride blinded him to their own love for him and to their own undeniable sacrifices for the truth. If Roger had any more light than they did, he did not yet have the wisdom to simply lift up a candle in the darkness as Winthrop had done those years before at Sempringham.

"I hold to it all," said Roger, as he looked from face to face around the room, "as I would to any doctrine of the Lord Jesus upon which you or I would gladly give our lives. But if I am guilty of tearing anything down, it is only because my heart burns for a heavenly city not made by hands, whose pattern we must strive to follow in all that we do!"

"I have no further questions, Governor," said Hooker sadly as he turned the proceedings back over to Haynes.

Two days later, Roger and the court met again. As Roger stood, Haynes read the court's sentence. Much of it seemed a dream to Roger, but the final words struck him with the force of a charging horse.

"Whereas Roger Williams has introduced and divulged various new and dangerous opinions against the authority of the magistrates and yet maintains these opinions without retracting them, he must depart from the Massachuseets Bay Colony within six weeks. If he fails to heed this order of expulsion, the magistrates have full authority to send him to some place out of this jurisdiction."

Banished! A man twice without a country. This was not just a dream; it was a nightmare.

But Roger was not a man given to despair.

The same month, Mary gave birth to her second child. They named the girl *Freeborn*.

"Mary, Mary," moaned Roger as he lay upon his sickbed in Salem, "bring me water, Dear! I'm so thirsty."

Mary lifted a pewter cup to his hot lips. "Drink, and then sleep, Darling," she whispered, as he lay back upon the piled pillows.

"I dreamed that I saw the bride of Christ, coming down out of heaven. Beautiful, she was, strong and pure and full of life," mumbled Roger with his eyes closed. "When will that day come? Why must these days be so full of stumbling and confusion?"

"Sleep, Darling," Mary repeated, as she wiped the silent tears from her own eyes. "Sleep, and dream of heaven."

"He always dream of heaven, whether he sleep or not," said a tall and powerful Indian who was standing beside the bed.

"Yes, you're right, Miantonomy." Mary smiled. "And that is why I love him."

"I love him, too," said the sachem, "but not because he dream of heaven. I love him for his love for me and for my Uncle Canonicus. I love him for his truth-speaking and his courage. Roger know God. God know Roger. God make him well again. Many things for him to do. Many people need him."

Mary touched the dark-skinned arm in thanks for Miantonomy's sincere words. She look with awed appreciation into his wild eyes, and then she left the room. Late that night Roger awakened briefly. In the darkness of his bedchamber, he could see the silhouetted form of a swarthy "guardian angel," kneeling in perfect stillness beside the bed. Miantonomy was keeping watch, perhaps praying silently on Roger's behalf to the radical preacher's Jesus.

Six weeks came and went. The Bay knew that Roger was ill, and so they didn't press for his immediate removal. In fact, they gave him until the next spring, provided he not try to draw others into agreement with his opinions. But as the weeks turned to months, they began to hear rumors that he was planning to start a colony around Narragansett Bay. They heard that twenty people were interested in joining him. Whether this was true or not, they could no longer afford to have this New England windmill grind out grain for bread that would poison their people.

They decided they must send him back to England, and a small ship was hired, under the command of Captain Underhill, to sail around to Salem and pack him off over the seas. But Roger had many friends in high places, and someone got the news to him before Underhill could carry out his orders. It was January of 1636, and the winter had been an incredibly wild and snowy one. When the captain finally hove into icy Salem harbor and trudged through the snow to knock on the door of Williams's house, Roger had been gone three days.

CHAPTER 8

1636

Even among the pines and under the tallest trees, the snow lay heavy. At woods edge and along frozen streams, it was drifted high. Rivers were hardened avenues of ice and crusted snow, and the frigid wind blew hard through the leafless forest. On this second day of Roger's wearied flight, a freezing rain fell with such sharpness that it threatened to cut the very bark from off the trees.

Fighting the bone-chilling cold and the feelings of despair and lostness that flew at him with each new wind-driven blast of winter rain, Roger forced himself through the white wilderness into the heart of the Wampanoag Country.

Though he well knew the way in fair weather, the landscape had been transformed by long and bitter months of hail and snow from heaven. It was only by the most obvious landmarks that Roger kept himself on the trail that he was following. But even now, his feverish mind was fighting to reach beyond this cold external world to a reality that transcended nature's times and seasons.

" 'Though your sins be as scarlet, they shall be as white as snow,' " Roger quoted to himself. "Where is my sin in standing for the truth, Lord God? What is this cleansing that drives me from my hearth and home, from my wife and children? Where is the fellowship of the brethren and the love of God in this vast, white land? If I live, I shall feel these moments 'til the day I die!"

Beside him, valiantly struggling through drifts that would frustrate a giant, was Roger's young domestic servant, Thomas Angell. Together, the thirty-three-year-old refugee and his fifteen-year-old servant slowly plowed a sixty-mile trail that nature quickly closed behind them. At this frozen moment in time, Roger couldn't possibly know the long trail that God had marked out for him to walk in the decades ahead. He had no inkling of his fuller destiny or calling. No desire whatever to be written into any chapters of anyone's history. No thoughts of tomorrow. As he stumbled desperately through the drifting landscape, he had only one thing in mind: the shelter of the tents of the Wampanoag Indians.

As they crossed the flat meadow country of the Wampanoags, the smoke from the wigwams of the town of Sowams came finally into view. Numbly, the ice-covered Englishmen staggered into the startled village. Barely able to return the greetings of the natives who met them, they were ushered to the home of the sachem, Massasoit. There, next to the fire of the Wampanoag chieftain, they fell in exhausted thankfulness upon the smokey mats and slept.

CHAPTER 9

1636

Within the warm tents of the Wampanoags, Roger was nursed to health. The youthful strength that had failed him during his time and ministry among his own, now returned in the quiet winter days among the Indians. He spoke often with them of God and His Son, but he never once confessed the reason for his strange sojourn through the bitter January storm. He sent word to Mary that he was well and that he would send for her soon. He also counseled long with Massasoit, and the two of them spoke of Roger's desire to settle near the Seekonk River on land that he had bought from Massasoit several years earlier.

"You bring your family there," said the sachem. "And some of your countrymen. You build your houses and plant your corn. And we will trade. We will be friends, Williams. I trust you. You speak true."

"If you need my help, I'll give it," said Roger. "If you need food and goods, I'll trade with you for them. If you wish to know the true God, I'll teach you and your sons and daughters about Him. And I'll live among you in peace, as God desires that we must."

When Roger was finally well enough to travel again, he and Angell crossed over the border into the Narragansett Country to visit with Canonicus.

"You are coming to live among us at last!" exclaimed the

aged sachem. "I am happy to see this day, for I love you as a son. You are more than English, Roger. You are like one who comes to all men as a friend. When you tell me of Jesus, I can think of no man like Him but you."

"I am honored that you would call me a son, Canonicus," said Roger, humbled and warmed at heart. He thought longingly of his own father and of Sir Edward Coke. "But I am not at all like the Savior. He is pure and righteous; I am full of sin."

"I am full of sin, too, my son," said the great chief. "My heart is one big stone. I pray to *Manìt*, and to your God's Son Jesus, that they will take my sin away. But perhaps my sin is stronger than yours, stronger even than the power of your Christ, because still it is within me. It always rises to darken my eyes."

"If we say we have no sin, we are liars, says God's book. But if we confess our sins, He is faithful and just to forgive us our sins," admonished Roger.

"What more does God want from me, Roger?" asked Canonicus sincerely.

"To turn from all the idols in your heart, in your worship, and in your life and to trust in Christ Jesus alone. Then you will be able to worship the true and living God," Roger replied.

Just before spring, Roger and Angell set out for the eastern shore of the Seekonk, to the spot that Roger and Massasoit had marked out years before. Here, the two companions raised a simple shelter and began to lay crops in the fertile ground. Here also they were joined by three men from Salem: a poor and destitute attorney's clerk named William Harris, a miller from Dorchester (also banished) named John Smith, and a poor young fellow named Francis Wicks. Though Roger desired a more hermitlike existence among the Indians, his heart was moved by these desperate men who had invited themselves to settle with him. He told them they could stay.

By now, the Bay had heard that Roger was alive. Good friends were much relieved, and most wished him well. But what many wished even more was that he was a wee bit farther away. Though Roger was on land he had purchased from Massasoit, he was also still within the jurisdiction of Plymouth. Roger's old friend Edward Winslow (now governor of Plymouth), not wanting any trouble with the Bay, sent a messenger advising Roger simply to cross to the other side of the river, so that he and Plymouth could freely live as loving neighbors. So Roger and his company left their half-planted crops in ground that Roger had bought for his own, and set their sights for the western shores of the Seekonk.

A slender canoe slipped down the wide river as the mid-April sun danced upon the ripples caused by the dipping, sliding oars. Along the shorelines, a huddle of Indians watched the five men slowly rowing. As the canoe came nearer, the leader of the white men shouted, "What cheer, *Nétop?*" and he motioned to the natives that he would be landing on the neck of ground just around the bend. The band of Indians followed as the canoe continued toward its destination.

At an outcropping of slate, Roger guided the boat into land. As he stood up in front of the canoe to lay hold on the rock, an Indian extended his hand. Red hand and white hand embraced in a clasp of friendship and greeting as Roger stepped onto the shore.

He smiled as the savages gathered curiously around him, then stared up into the azure spring sky.

"By God's mercy and providence, He has been with me in my distress," confessed Roger aloud. "I sense His presence in this place. Should Canonicus sell me land on these shores, I shall call this place Providence."

CHAPTER 10

1636

Winthrop closed the inside shutters of his study window, turned the wick up higher in his lamp, and sat down at his desk. An election in May (that had won Sir Henry Vane the Massachusetts governorship over John Haynes) had restored Winthrop to power by giving him the seat of second in command. Now, as deputy governor, he had an urgent message to pen. Taking out his ink and sharpening his quill, he pulled a sheet of parchment from his desk drawer. A small stack of letters within the drawer caught his attention, and he took them out. They were letters from Roger, written from Providence over the past several months. Winthrop opened the first one he had received:

> *It was not price or money that purchased Providence. 'Tis true Canonicus received many presents and gifts from me, but neither a thousand nor ten thousand dollars could have bought from him an English entrance into his land. He is very wary of the English, though not in the least afraid of us. No amount of money could have bought Providence, or any other land I have from him. Providence was purchased by love.*

"May that love, and indeed the providence of God, serve

us in this dark hour!" said Winthrop.

He opened another letter:

It is not true that I was hired by any, or made covenant with any, or desired that anyone come with me into this wilderness. But they have come, and I have yielded to their interest to settle here. I have rented out portions of my land to those who will have it, and I have ordered that no man be molested for his conscience. If nowhere else, men may come to Providence and be free.

"Roger, dear Roger, your soft heart will call down trouble upon your hard head! For soon every heretic and moral rebel will be knocking at your door," Winthrop commented. "But we must lock our doors and take up arms if we are to be truly free in these frightful days."

Then he slipped Roger's latest letter from its envelope. It was dated October 7, 1636. Yesterday.

The Pequot Indians, seemingly as evil as their father Satan, have determined to annihilate the English. Only days ago they attacked and murdered several of our countrymen outside Saybrook Fort on the Connecticut River. The war between the Pequots and the Narragansetts being at an end, and peace now promised between the two, the Pequots have sent ambassadors to Miantonomy. They wish to form an alliance with sachem and his uncle against the English, to push us back into the

sea. I pray God will have mercy upon us and frus-
trate all their counsels.

"May God have mercy indeed, friend Williams!" said
Winthrop with resolve. "And may He use you and your bond
of love with the Narragansett chiefs to do the frustrating!"

The deputy set the letters to one side, dipped his quill
into the inkpot, and began to write:

Dear Roger,
On behalf of the governor of Massachusetts and his
assistants, I am asking you to put your life into
God's hand in the errand of the utmost import.

When Roger received the message from Winthrop, he did
not hesitate. Scarcely acquainting his wife with his desperate
assignment, he set off immediately. . .and alone. A hazardous
thirty-mile voyage over troubled waters would take him to
his destination: the great wigwam city of Canonicus.

The dark waters of the Narragansett Bay danced violently
to the shrill song of the howling fall wind. Roger plowed
through the cold, salty waves, forcing his oar through the water
on one side of his canoe and then on the other. The little boat
rose and fell like a ship on a tempest-tossed sea. As the long
hours passed and the city of the great sachem finally came into
view, Roger cried out in weary thanks for God's protection
and prayed for His help in the task ahead. When Roger hove
up on the shores of Canonicus's capital, the hand of God was
as strong upon him as the heavy surf that had soaked him to
the skin.

The sight of this storm-blasted Englishman, striding tall and full of purpose, caused many of the natives to shrink back as Roger entered the packed statehouse where the convincing Pequots were parleying with Canonicus and Miantonomy.

"What this English doing here?" demanded the head Pequot ambassador.

"Why not ask him yourself?" said Miantonomy gravely. But Canonicus simply motioned for Roger to take a seat near the fire.

"We are talking of a pact together," the grand sachem said to Roger. "One which would unite our peoples against any further trespassing of the English. And of course, that is why you have come, is it not?"

"That is why I have come," Roger replied.

For three days and nights Roger lodged with the Indians, counseling with Canonicus, reasoning with Miantonomy, arguing against the appeals of the Pequots, and pleading instead for an alliance between the English and the Narragansetts. All the while, he imagined he could smell the blood of his countrymen upon the hands and arms of the Pequot ambassadors. Nightly, he expected them to put a knife to his throat. But God wondrously protected him and helped him at last to shatter the Pequots' plans. Miantonomy was quickly won to Roger's cause, but Canonicus was a harder case.

"I have never decreed any wrong be done to the English since he landed," declared Canonicus. "And as long as the Englishman speaks true, then I shall go to my grave in peace. But if he speaks lies, if he takes what belongs to me and my people, I will not stand aside. I will do all I can to stop him."

"But you have no cause to question the Englishman's

faithfulness," replied Roger. "You have had long experience of his friendliness and trustiness." Though some English, as well as French and Dutch, had treated the Indians unfairly, even treacherously, Roger knew that the Bay had always pursued a Christian policy of peace and respect toward its Indian neighbors.

Canonicus picked up a stick near the fire and broke it in ten pieces. He then related ten instances (laying down a piece of stick with each instance) that gave him cause to doubt the Englishman's faithfulness.

Roger did his best to address each grievance and promised to present Canonicus's case to the English governors. For Roger's sake, and through the wisdom and sincerity of his pleas, the aged chieftain declared himself satisfied. He broke off the Pequot negotiations and agreed instead to an alliance with the Bay!

When war between the Pequots and the English broke out later that year, Miantonomy and the Narragansett braves fought on the side of the Bay. The Pequots were defeated and were never again a threat to any man.

God had used Roger to bring about a victory that enabled the whole land, English and natives, to sleep in peace securely. And though the Bay blessed God for Roger's unselfish courage and service to them in the conflict, his unrepentant Separatism would forever keep them apart. The banishment was not lifted.

CHAPTER 11

1637–1650

The years following the Pequot War saw Providence beginning to swell with an influx of new settlers: seekers, Separatists, Baptists, dissidents, and the discontent. Roger purchased more land from Canonicus, including the Islands of Rhode and Aquidneck in the Narragansett Bay, and he tried to divvy it up equally to all who came.

But Winthrop's prediction of trouble rang all too true. Many who came to Roger's spiritual haven were far more concerned for themselves than for any great godly principles. They were more interested in license than in liberty. They were more intent on building their personal kingdoms than in seeking the kingdom of God.

There were constant squabbles over the land. New towns (Newport, Pawtuxet, and Portsmouth) sprung up, with their own governments, simply because folks couldn't get along. Roger was continually busy being "Moses" to a band of grumbling "Israelites."

He wrote often to Winthrop, who was governor once again, sharing his concerns and asking for advice. Winthrop did all that he could to help Roger "build his house on rock," but he was sincerely troubled by the growing community of spiritual oddballs and doctrinal outlaws.

Meanwhile, Massachusetts, Plymouth, and Connecticut all began to look longingly southward toward the fertile, unchartered lands upon which Roger had settled. Within Roger's own borders, a man named William Arnold carved a large piece of Roger's pie for himself and then gave it to Massachusetts!

If the new settlements south of the Seekonk were to survive as an independent colony alongside the older English plantations, they must have something more than land deeds from the Indians (which the English did not recognize as legal). They must have a Royal Charter. The Assembly at Newport voted to look into the possibility of an English patent for Rhode Island and the lands adjacent. Their choice of an agent to be sent to England on their behalf was, of course, Roger Williams.

Roger bid farewell to his family and friends and set sail for England in March of 1643. During his voyage, he wrote a small book about the Narragansett Indians and their language and customs. He named it *A Key into the Language of America*. He compiled it as a help to his own memory and to many who had asked him for assistance in their temporal and spiritual dealings with the natives. It was published in London upon his arrival in September and became an instant hit, making Roger famous overnight.

Parliament had been reinstated by King Charles and then dissolved by him a second time. Parliament then reconvened itself on behalf of the people of England and proceeded to declare war against the king. The civil war had begun only a year earlier in 1642, making it very difficult for Roger to find a listening ear for his problems across the seas. So he bided his time by entering the religious and political fray. He wrote many pamphlets in support of freedom of religion and against persecution of one's faith. He argued for an English government that encouraged differences in matters of faith but that kept its hands out of church matters. He argued for a church that was pure and holy and that kept itself free from the influence of the world. And he argued for a truce between the two that would allow all Englishmen to worship as their consciences dictated.

He wrote: "In many ways (not spiritual), the church or gathering of worshipers, whether it is a true church or not, is like a Physicians' Society, a Merchants' Company, and East Indies Tea Corporation, or any other society or company in London. Each of these societies holds its own meetings, keeps its own records, and goes about the concerns of its business. Its members may disagree, divide, form separate companies, sue each other at law, even break up and dissolve into nothing, and still the peace of the city is not in the least disturbed.

"Surely a church can be allowed to operate in the same way," said Roger. "Let each church, whether a true church or not, declare its own purposes and judge its own affairs. As to the Truth itself, it does not need the protection of the sword, nor can it be furthered by the sword. God's Spirit alone can reveal it, and God's power alone will preserve it! For God is Truth."

Most people thought this reasoning very strange, but Roger's words challenged them to reexamine their understanding of both church and state. Roger was primarily arguing for the purity of the Church of Jesus Christ, and he had no way of knowing that he was also helping to lay the foundation for a freer, more democratic society that would one day come forth in England and (much sooner) in America.

Finally, in March of 1944, Parliament granted Roger an official charter of Providence Plantations.

In September of 1644, Roger was jubilantly welcomed home to Providence. The general outpouring of affection and appreciation warmed his heart, but it was tempered by the tragic news that his friend Miantonomy had been murdered by the Mohicans shortly after Roger had left for England.

"A giant has fallen," Roger murmured as he heard the grisly tale, and his mind wandered back to a day in his childhood, the day Bartholemew Legate was burned. As he had wondered then whether the heretic Legate had gone to heaven or to hell, so now he was burdened with fear for the eternal destiny of Miantonomy's soul. How he hated the barbaric spirit and fierce pride that held so many of the natives in chains of darkness! He could almost hear his father's words: "Though I hate his heresy for the heresy it is. . ." Heresy or heathenism, what is the difference? Both lead to weeping and wailing and gnashing of teeth in the world beyond this one. ". . .he had been a friend!" A friend. A true friend.

Had Roger's friend Miantonomy ever truly trusted in Christ? Would he ever see his friend again?

The whole town assembled to hear the reading of the charter. After much public and private discussion, Providence accepted it as written, and Roger was immediately elected as chief officer of the new colony. The other three towns were much slower in agreeing to a unified government: It took them almost three years! But in May of 1647, all four towns finally organized themselves into one united body. Roger, feeling his part in the political salvation of the colony had been fully played, breathed a thankful sigh of relief, turned in his resignation, and headed for the woods. He was forty-four years old.

Canonicus was fading fast. The brave old prince had seen his last sunrise and had sent a messenger running to Roger early in the day.

"I have asked my white son to close my eyes in death," Canonicus said feebly to the men and women who stood by his bed. "But I had hoped to see him once again before that hour."

Turning to the sachem who would rule after him, Canonicus gave this charge, "Live with Roger Williams in love and peace all your days. If war should ever come with the English, see that no Narragansett ever harm a hair of Roger's head."

When Roger arrived in the early evening, the women and the girls were wailing, their faces and clothes blackened with soot. The men lay weeping on thick piles of darkened ashes. The mournful cries of *"Kitonckquei!* (He is dead!)" and *"Nipwi maw!* (He is gone!)" could be heard throughout the city.

Roger walked solemnly into the death chamber of Canonicus. With unrestrained tears streaming down his cheeks, he looked one last time into the dark, vacant eyes of the great chieftain. As an assembly of mourners gathered around, Roger gently placed his fingers on the eyelids of the dead sachem. With one motion, he closed those eyes that had been open for so long and had seen so much. They had seen the birth and death of many sons and daughters. They had seen the rise and fall of many Indian nations. They had seen the coming of the white man's ships. They had seen, and understood, the beginning of the end of the Narragansetts themselves.

Roger rose, and the mourners fell weeping upon the mats within the wigwam.

"How dreadful is the death of the unbelieving," muttered Roger as he wandered back into the forest toward his home. "And yet, when the hearts of my countrymen and friends failed me, God's infinite wisdom and merits stirred up the barbarous heart of Canonicus to love me as his son to his last gasp."

In a small, sunlit clearing about six miles from Providence, Roger built his trading house. Within sight of the sturdy log house was a quiet cove where a small pinnace was anchored. Pulled up on shore were several smaller boats and canoes.

Many trails led inland to the neighboring Indian villages (with twenty villages to a mile in some cases), and Roger's little house was constantly humming with the healthy activity of frontier trade.

For the Indians, Roger kept a full stock of everything they needed: pans, kettles, knives, cooking utensils of all sorts, spades, hoes, and other gardening equipment, cloth, pins, needles, thread, beads, trinkets, and toys. But the items in largest demand were tobacco and pipes to smoke it in. Nobody then knew, as we now do, that tobacco was dangerous, and so Roger had a ready supply at all times. The one thing he would not carry, that the natives craved even over tobacco, was whiskey. Though he could have made a fortune (as other less scrupulous traders did) in the sale of alcohol, he loved the Indians too much to sell them something that could destroy them.

Though these were busy days for Roger, it was a quiet sort of busyness. And though his trading post and his farm in Providence provided well for his household, the trading post also provided something far nearer his heart: a pulpit from which to preach. "Preaching is the best of all callings," Roger said, "but a poor trade." So he did both. His Indian customers were his parish, and he preached to them often. And not just on Sundays.

Sometimes Roger's wife Mary would come from their home in Providence to be with him and help him in his work. Sometimes his two oldest daughters, Mary and Freeborn, would be with him (there were now six Williams children growing up in the Providence home). Sometimes he labored alone. During this time, he wrote a little spiritual devotional for his wife, entitled *Experiments of Spiritual Life and Health*. Unlike most of his other writings, it was not at all controversial and was full of practical encouragement for living the Christian life.

In the year 1649, two great men died.

One died an old man, peacefully in his bed in the New World, leaving behind him a legacy of godliness, temperance, and a spiritual, moral, and governmental foundation upon which a unique and mighty nation would be built.

The other died in the prime of his life, violently on a scaffold in the Old World, leaving behind him a record of royal fortitude, personal courage, and a doomed struggle to revive an ancient, outmoded philosophy of English life.

The man in his bed was John Winthrop, and all of New

England mourned his passing.

The man on the scaffold was King Charles the First, and though many rejoiced at his fall, much of England groaned. More was severed than the king's neck with the swift blow of the executioner's axe. Broken forever in that instant was England's unthinking submission to the crown. What England's new leader, Oliver Cromwell, called "cruel necessity" was the dim beginning of a society governed by the people and for the people. But it was a harsh genesis. And it was a long crawl toward true freedom. England's Puritans now had the chance to rule in Old England. It wouldn't be easy.

In Providence, Roger wept for the passing of a man in Boston. Though Winthrop had been among those who had banished him, the two had been through much together. Roger would miss him dearly, though they would meet again in a longer, brighter day. He wept also for the death of a man in London, for he knew the man's deeds had been wicked.

Both men would stand before God to give an account for their lives.

"This life is but a brief minute," said Roger quietly. "Eternity follows."

1675

It was a black page in New England history. A war of shame for both red man and white. Fear and distrust, self-righteousness and revenge, ruled in men's hearts. Prudence and promises were trampled underfoot as drums beat and arrows flew and muskets bellowed.

Much blood was shed, and much of it innocent blood— blood of Indian and Englishman alike. But all of it red as it soaked the common soil.

English settlers were killed in their sleep, whole families massacred. Homes were burned. Towns were burned. Cattle were destroyed. Crops were ravaged.

Indian warriors and helpless old men and women were slaughtered in a tragic winter battle that needn't have been fought. The Narragansett tribe was reduced to near extinction.

In Rhode Island (as Providence Plantation was now called), Roger desperately tried to convince the pacifist Quaker government of Providence to fortify the town. But they would not. The town of Warwick was burned on March 17, and on March 26, the marauding Wampanoag Indians arrived at Providence.

As the native force approached the town, they were met by a white-haired seventy-three-year-old man who was leaning on a staff. He called out to them, saying that he would parley with them. They spoke with him for an hour, but he was unable to dissuade them from their dreadful purpose. Roger Williams's influence meant nothing on that fatal day. Most of Providence, including Roger's home and all his worldly goods, were burned to the ground. Only twenty-three houses out of 103 remained. But no one touched as much of a hair on Roger's head.

Four months later, King Philip (Metacomet, son of Massasoit), the bitter sachem who had incited and led the massive Indian uprising, was slain in a swamp by a former member of his tribe. Sixteen days later, the war ended at Annawan Rock on the eastern side of the Seekonk River.

New England would rise again from the ashes, stronger and more determined than ever to follow its destiny to the ends of an empire. Not so the tribes that had filled its tall forest; they would diminish as the years went by, like trees growing backwards from maturity to saplings, and then to mere weeds lost amidst the rocks and ferns.

1683

"Mary," said Roger weakly.

"Yes, Dearest," whispered his tender wife and faithful companion.

"Have you anything you wish me to say to Winthrop when I see him?" asked Roger.

"To Winthrop?" said Mary hesitantly. Then she laughed gently, for surely Roger was dreaming. Old John Winthrop had been dead for over thirty years. But then her face grew solemn, and she stood up from her chair and walked over to the bed where Roger lay.

"Roger," she said sadly and softly, "tell him he was wrong."

"Kitonckquei," they said, in the depleted villages of Narragansetts. And those who had known him smeared themselves with soot.

"He is dead," they said, in the towns and on the trails of New England. And those who had known him bowed their heads in prayer.

"Oh, how terrible is the look, the speedy and serious thought of death to all the sons of men!" he himself once wrote. "Thrice happy are those who are dead and risen with the Son of God, for they are passed from death to life, and shall never see death again!"

The town of Providence turned out in unison in a vast parade that followed Roger's body to its burial. A final loud salute was raised as guns were fired over the grave. Red and white, Christian and Jew, heretic and heathen: All stood together on the hallowed ground. Some wept. Some wondered. Their united peaceful presence there was all the honor Roger would have wished for.

ABRAHAM LINCOLN

THE GREAT EMANCIPATOR

by Sam Wellman

CHAPTER 1

"Can I go explore now, Father?" asked Abe.

Tom Lincoln stopped chopping wood with an axe and gave Abe a stern look. "*If* you finished your chores, you can go play. But don't go down near the creek!"

Abe glanced down at Knob Creek. White water boiled over and around the rocks. He looked up a slope toward cliffs that shot straight up to the sky. The cliffs were dotted with stout cedar trees. Abe trudged up the slope.

Today, another boy explored the slope above the log cabin where Abe lived. The boy wore yellow pants made from deer hide like Abe's father wore. Deer hide was called buckskin. The boy in buckskin put his fists on his hips and growled, "I'm Austin. What's your name, shirttail boy?"

"I'm Abe." All his life, Abe had never worn pants at all. He wore a long itchy shirt that came to his knees. He never thought the shirt was unusual until now.

Austin squinted. "How come I've never seen you before? How old are you?"

"Thanks for asking." Abe loved to tell stories, and this was one of his favorites. "I was born one morning over on Rock Spring farm. My sister Sarah woke up and saw Father standing by the bed. Mother was in a heap of bearskins on the bed. She was holding a wrinkly red baby in a blanket. Sarah said my eyes and fists were closed tighter than walnuts. Black hair already plastered my head. Mother said 'Let's name this boy Abraham after your father, Tom. . .' "

"How old are you?" asked Austin impatiently.

"I was born to Nancy and Tom Lincoln on the Lord's Day, February 12 in the year 1809. . ."

"This is 1814. You're only five? You're as big as me, and I'm seven. Can you wrestle, shirttail boy?" Austin's hands became spidery, ready to grab Abe.

"Like this?" Abe wrestled Austin to the ground. He let Austin get up right away. He knew when he wrestled Sarah, if he held her down very long she got really mad.

Austin grinned. "Yes. Like that. When are you coming to school, Abe?"

"What do you do at school?"

"I learn reading and writing and ciphering. Ciphering is adding up and subtracting numbers."

Abe shrugged. "I know all twenty-six letters of the alphabet. I can count to a hundred. I can't go to school anyway. I have chores to do. I carry water. I fill the wood box. I hoe weeds. I slop the hogs. I poke seeds of corn into plowed ground. I fetch tools for Father. . . ."

Austin interrupted him, "I get the idea: You're not coming to school."

And the boys played hide-and-seek in a field of corn.

A few days after Abe met Austin, Tom Lincoln hitched two horses to their big wagon. Tom lifted Abe into the wagon. Abe asked suspiciously, "Are you taking me to school?"

"No. We're going to Elizabethtown."

In Elizabethtown, Abe saw a man with black skin being worked like a mule. The man wore a collar around his neck. The man's eyes never left the ground. Tom explained the black man was a slave owned by the mill owner.

Abe noticed something. His father's voice was cheerful and light when he had been telling funny stories in front of the general store. Now his voice was sad and heavy—like the time they found their hog chewed up by a bear.

Abe asked, "How can a man own another man?"

Tom grunted. "It's the law here in Kentucky. All black folks in Kentucky are slaves."

Abe looked up and down the street. He saw lots of black folks—black women and children too. "What's law?"

"Rules white men make up."

"What's Kentucky?"

Tom had to laugh. "Elizabethtown here and the farm where we live are inside the state called Kentucky. There are seventeen other states in the United States. That's the nation we live in. Israel in the good book is a nation."

All the way home, Abe thought about law and states and nations and slaves. Things were simple on their farm. Abe knew how to make soap and candles. He saw how his mother ground corn into cornmeal, then baked it to make bread. He saw how his father, Tom, took rough walnut logs and made them into a smooth corner cabinet. But away from the farm Abe knew almost nothing. How would he ever know these things?

Every Sunday, the Lincolns walked to Little Mount Church. Preacher Elkins talked from the good book about the good news that Jesus had died and come alive again. But then the preacher closed the good book and frowned as he talked about how bad folks were who owned slaves.

When Abe or Sarah made them late to church, Abe could hear Preacher Elkins preaching even though they were still a long way off. Preacher Elkins could talk softly, too. And Abe watched how the preacher used his arms. Once in awhile, the preacher would throw his arms high, raise right up on his toes, and boom his voice off the ceiling.

On the way home, Tom would say, "Mighty powerful preaching today. . ."

Mother would add, "No one can preach like Preacher Elkins."

One morning after a breakfast of eggs and bacon, Abe's mother said, "Abe has been shirttail boy long enough."

Tom didn't go outside to do chores like he usually did after breakfast. He grinned and said, "This I have to see."

"Here, Abe." Mother held up a pair of pants!

Abe fell down twice trying to get them on. Finally, he sat on a bench and tugged them on. The pants were made from yellow buckskin like Austin's. But Abe's pants were new and spotless. When he walked around in them, they felt stiff and very heavy. He felt like he was wading through water.

Mother said, "Put on your moccasins, Abe."

"Why? It didn't snow." Then he noticed Sarah was wearing a new dress. It was made of a kind of cotton cloth Mother called calico. Abe muttered, "What's going on?"

Tom said, "Let's get going. It's two miles away. I'll give you a ride the first day."

Abe asked, "What's two miles away?"

Sarah laughed. "School, fancy pants."

"It's a blab school," said Mother.

Abe rode in the wagon with Tom and Sarah to the rough cabin that was a school. Inside, Abe saw Austin jabbering out of a book. All twenty boys and girls sat on benches and jabbered lessons out loud at the same time so that the teacher would know they were working.

Abe blurted, "So that's why Mother calls it a blab school."

Abe already knew the alphabet. It wasn't long before he blabbed words from a thin book called a Speller. After one month, he blabbed from the Speller a whole sentence of one-syllable words, "Trust in the Lord with all your heart."

His teacher said, "That's a proverb, right out of the Bible."

"My mother reads that same proverb out of the good book we have at home."

That fact hit Abe like a bolt of lightning! At home that night he began to read the good book. On the very first page, it said the good book was God's greatest gift!

Every night, the Lincolns sat together in front of the fireplace. While his mother read from the Bible, Abe studied her. She was thin and very tall. Dark brown hair was parted in the middle. Her face looked winkled and hollow. She was missing some teeth. She had a high forehead and yellow-brown eyes. Long ago, when she was still called Nancy Hanks, his mother must have looked like Sarah.

And while his father told stories of every kind, Abe sized him up. Tom wasn't much taller than Mother. But his shoulders were wide, his arms thick. Abe wasn't like him that way. Abe was thin and gawky. When Abe peered at himself in a mud puddle, the only things that looked like they belonged on his father were his coarse black hair and deep-set gray eyes.

There were silent times by the fire, too. Mother sewed. Tom cleaned his carpenter tools. Abe and Sarah did spelling and grammar lessons from their Speller. The Speller used examples from the Bible. For Abe and Sarah the good book was everywhere. God's Word was as basic to their lives as air. They never ate a meal before Tom said, "Fit and prepare us for humble service for Christ's sake. Amen."

Abe practiced writing, too. Paper was far too precious to use. If he was in front of the fire, he blacked words on firewood with a piece of charcoal. If he was outside the cabin, he fingered words in the dirt or mud or snow.

But sometimes he just had fun exploring with Austin.

One time Abe's father had been gone on a trip nearly a month. Wintry clouds had been scraping the cliff tops, and it had been raining hard for a week. One morning the sun shone again. So Abe explored along the banks of Knob Creek with Austin. The water in Knob Creek didn't boil around the rocks like it usually did. No rocks could be seen at all.

Abe said, "The water looks calm."

"The water only looks calm because it's so deep and muddy. It's swifter than it's ever been." Austin sounded scared. "Look. It cut into the bank and knocked that old birch tree over."

"The tree toppled right across Knob Creek!" yelled Abe. "It's a bridge!" He jumped up on the dark scaly bark. "We can see what's over on the other side."

Austin cried, "You better not! You can't swim!"

Abe slipped. The last thing he saw before he thrashed into the creek was Austin's mouth drop open in horror.

CHAPTER 2

Icy water yanked Abe along like a hundred horses. He clawed weeds at the bank's edge as he was swept by.

He saw Austin running along the bank beside him. The creek rolled Abe over. Water rushed into his nose. Pain stung below his eyes and inside his forehead. He tried to scream. Water choked him. He kicked a rock with his toe. He was sinking. He prayed, "Oh, please save me, Jesus. . . ."

Abe beat his arms against the crushing water. His fingers touched something. He grabbed.

He held something! If only he could pull himself to the bank. But he was too weak. He would never make it. He couldn't breathe. Everything was spinning, going black.

Something whacked him on the back. He gagged. The creek gushed from his throat. Again and again he gagged. His back hurt. His stomach ached. His throat burned.

"Wake up, Abe!" It was Austin's voice.

Abe opened his eyes. He was on the bank, a branch by his face. He sputtered, "I. . .I. . .I'm alive."

Austin said, "It's a good thing you grabbed that branch so I could haul you in."

Abe shivered from more than cold. It was quite awhile before he said, "I came one branch from dying."

"It was more than a branch," said Austin. "It was like your mother always says: 'God has a plan for you, Abe.' "

Abe was silent. He wasn't sure Austin was right. Could a boy be so foolish he could actually defeat God's plan? It was something very important to think about.

Three weeks before Christmas, his father Tom returned from his trip. That first night back, while all four Lincolns warmed in front of a fire roaring in the fireplace, Tom said, "We are going to move to a new state called Indiana."

Mother explained, "Father and I decided we have to leave Kentucky. Our neighbors are buying more and more slaves. In Indiana, no man can be made a slave."

Abe knew Indiana must be someplace special.

Into the big wagon they loaded everything they owned except their furniture. It was easier for Tom to make new furniture at their new home. Two horses pulled the wagon. Tied behind the wagon were two more horses and one cow. Three hounds chased each other around the wagon.

Abe was scared when he climbed up into the wagon box. But he didn't complain. Tom turned on the wagon seat to say, "I'm sorry you children are cold. But winter is the best time to move. We're living off food we salted and dried anyway. And these roads are frozen solid as rock instead of being knee-deep in mud."

They clopped along the frozen mud road mile after mile. Chickens clucked in wooden cages, and hogs grunted right next to Abe. He was sad as he remembered all the times he and Austin had played together. Would he ever see Austin again?

The wagon stopped. . . .

"I never saw such a thing!" shouted Sarah.

The gleaming ribbon of water was ten times wider than Abe could skip a flat rock. Tom laughed. "Only the men on the barges, flatboats, and big steamboats know how many times deeper than Abe's nose that Ohio River is."

Mother beamed. "On the other side is Indiana."

A ferryboat took them across the Ohio River, and they headed the wagon into woods folks called "rough." Indiana had rough like Abe had never seen before. Oak, sycamore, hackberry, ash, poplar, maple, and beech trees towered into the sky. Grapevines as thick as small trees webbed all the trees and undergrowth together.

"A snake has to work hard to squeeze through this rough," joked Tom. But he had to hack and chop from dawn to dusk, day after day, to clear the way for the wagon.

Tom seemed to relax after they reached a high area. He said, "This land is just above Little Pigeon Creek."

"Look. A half-face." Abe pointed at a crude, three-sided lean-to called a half-faced camp. The walls were made of logs and boughs. The fourth side was open. "Someone lives here," said Abe.

"I built that." Tom waved around them. "This is the land I claimed."

Abe jumped out of the wagon. "So this is where you were while you were gone."

Tom nodded. "I stacked brush on each corner to mark our claim. The corners mark a square one-half mile on each side. Our land is rich in oak and hickory trees. Natural salt licks attract all kinds of wild critters. Springs seep good water north of the half-face. Over yonder to the east, there's a small stream moseying right across our land."

The three hounds were already learning the new property. Abe heard them way off somewhere in the tangled rough, baying and yelping.

Tom smiled. "Within one year, I have to ride up to the

town of Vincennes. I have to pay $80 to the government to get a paper that proves we own this 160 acres." He frowned. "We'll still owe them $240."

Abe whistled. "This land cost two whole dollars per acre!"

Mother said, "Let's get settled. Abe, unload a bag of corn-meal and a ham for supper. Sarah, spread leaves over the ground in the half-face."

Tom grabbed his axe. "I'll take care of the animals."

Tom build a shelter and corral for the horses and the cow. The sky was dark as he finished a separate one for the hogs. He saw Abe had moved the cages full of chickens into the half-face. A big fire had to be kept blazing there all the time in place of a fourth wall.

Tom said, "We'll build a chicken coop tomorrow, then we'll start the cabin. We have two sharp axes."

Two axes! It was the first night Abe didn't fall asleep think-ing how much he missed Austin. Under wool blankets and bearskins, with hens clucking softly by his head, Abe dreamed of swinging the axe. Sometime in the night the hounds re-turned, panting and exhausted.

The next morning Tom said, "Let's get started." He handed seven-year-old Abe an axe.

Tom chopped down trees one foot thick that could be cut into logs twenty feet long. They needed thirty-two of these logs, eight for each wall. Abe whacked off the limbs. He notched the ends, so the logs would lock together.

They cut shorter logs for the gables, the uppermost triangle-shaped parts of the walls at each end of the cabin. They made a nice sloping roof by overlapping wood shingles on thin logs that stretched from gable to gable. Inside the cabin, Tom placed beams from wall to wall eight feet above the floor. He pounded stout wood pegs up one wall.

Abe asked, "Why do you need those pegs?"

"You and Sarah will need them."

Abe shrugged. "What for?"

Tom laughed. "To climb up to the loft I'm going to build on the beams. That's where you and Sarah will sleep."

Abe and Sarah "chinked" thin slabs of wood in the cracks between the logs. After chinking, they daubed mud between the logs. To Abe the cabin was wonderful. His family made it right out of the forest. It was solid and safe and smelled of fresh-cut wood.

Abe bragged, "We made the cabin in just four days."

"With God's mercy," said Mother.

"You handled an axe like a man, Abe." Tom looked puzzled, just like the time Mother convinced him Abe was really reading the Bible and not reciting it from memory.

Sarah scanned the thick rough woods around the cabin. "When are we going back to school?"

Tom said, "Folks can't get a teacher to come here yet. You can school yourself."

Abe practiced reading and writing every morning. A neighbor told Tom he wanted to write his mother in Kentucky but didn't know how to write. Tom told him maybe Abe could write a letter for him. So Abe not only wrote the letter but worked out the very best way to write what the neighbor wanted to say. Soon other neighbors asked Abe to write letters for them. Tom heard folks at Gentry's Store talking about how Abe was ahead of other boys his age. He was taller. He could write, and he could swing an axe!

Before the next winter, Abe's aunt and uncle, the Sparrows, and their son Dennis Hanks, moved from Kentucky to live near the Lincolns. Although Dennis was several years older than Abraham, the two cousins became friends. When they found time, seventeen-year-old Dennis and Abe talked as equals: Dennis, an older fun-loving joker, and Abe, a younger wizard that folks talked about.

Tom Lincoln got a copy of *Aesop's Fables*. Abe read it through and through. The fables weren't as deep and moving as the parables Jesus told in the Bible, but a fable like a fox and the grapes was fun to read. Abe loved how fables and parables helped him understand life better. He turned stories inside and out, up and down, front and back. None of the Lincolns got much sleep any night because Abe kept talking about what a fable or a parable meant.

"Jumping Jehoshaphat," exclaimed Tom. "I never saw anyone chew on an idea like you, Abe. You're like an Indian woman chewing deer hide until it's soft. You won't let go of it until you've got it exactly the way it's supposed to be."

Mother added, "The only time Abe loses his temper is when he doesn't understand something he reads or hears."

Once in awhile now, Abe got to ride a horse alone to the mill. He took a bag of corn to grind into flour. The mill was the kind where the customer had to use his own horse to grind the corn. Abe hitched his horse to the beam and began strolling behind the horse on its endless circular path. It seemed like it would take forever.

"Get up, you old horse!" he yelled without thinking.

The frightened horse whinnied.

As quickly as a flick of the horse's tail, everything went black for Abe.

CHAPTER 3

Abe drifted through space too black and too deep to ever put in words.

He heard a man cry, "I can't get a pulse! The poor boy is dead!"

Abe opened his eyes. He was looking at the sky. Where was the horse? He felt the pebbly ground sticking in his back.

A whiskery face looked down at him. "Abe's alive!" The face belonged to the owner of the mill.

Abe asked, "What happened, Mr. Gordon?"

Mr. Gordon pressed a wet rag against Abe's forehead. "You just lay down for a spell. Your horse almost plumb kicked your head off, Abe." He whispered to someone, "I was sure Abe was dead."

After awhile Abe got up. A huge lump on his forehead throbbed pain with every heartbeat. As he rode the horse home, he recited verses memorized from the Bible. His mind worked all right. He didn't like to think about what had happened. That was the second time he almost died.

Tom Lincoln got Abe and Sarah a copy of *Pilgrim's Progress*. Abe read *Pilgrim's Progress* again and again, just like other books. It told of a pilgrim's journey to save his soul from hell. The pilgrim survived one disaster after another and succeeded despite constant danger. Abe's own life on the frontier didn't always seem dangerous, but that made it even more dangerous. One careless moment could end his life. He remembered the horse at the mill.

At the front of the book was a sketch of the life of the Englishman who wrote the book. Abe read that John Bunyan was "raised from the deepest obscurity. . .to be uncommonly useful for mankind." Every time Abe read that passage, his heart pounded so hard he had to stop.

He prayed, "How could anyone be more obscure than I am out here in the woods? Maybe I too can be uncommonly useful. Is that Your plan for me, God?" Yet he knew how Bunyan's pilgrim suffered one disaster after another. Was that God's plan for Abe? Things were very pleasant right now on their farm. Every night he talked with his family and read in front of the fire. And he heard folks had found a teacher. Abe might even get some schooling once in awhile.

Abe loved his job in the forest. Someday corn would stretch far beyond their cabin. Abe's job was to chop out bushes and grapevines growing under the trees. Tom was always within shouting distance. But Abe felt like he worked alone. He knew other folks were working just like him all around the forest. He imagined how they all cleared land farther and farther away from their cabins. Would the day ever come when they would all break out of the forest suddenly and he would see neighbors standing everywhere?

Abe was never really alone. The forest chattered and squeaked and bellowed with critters. It was a rare day a flock of passenger pigeons didn't darken the sky. Squirrels scolded him from the trees. Skunks ambled by fearlessly, armed with sting-ing smell. Wildcats hissed but were never seen. Blue-skinned lizards darted away. Snakes slithered under leaves. Wasps buzzed him from papery nests.

"Jumping Jehoshaphat," he mimicked his father. "How

you critters can carry on."

The second summer in Indiana was not like the first summer. Tom grumbled, "It's too hot. It's too dry. I don't like this. Hot, dry summers are not good."

Abe said, "It's not so bad if you go swimming now and again." Abe heard about the local swimming hole on Little Pigeon Creek from Dennis Hanks. Abe was always hinting that he should be allowed to go there, too.

Abe's mother and father exchanged worried looks. Abe thought they worried about him swimming.

One late summer evening, Tom was too quiet by the fire. His face, so darkened by the sun, looked white. Finally he said, "I think our old cow has got the trembles."

"Trembles!" Mother, who was always calm, had to calm herself before she asked, "Are you sure she isn't just old?"

Tom replied softly, "We'll wait and see. Nobody drink any milk or eat any cheese. Go to bed, children."

And Tom left the cabin for awhile.

Abe and Sarah climbed into the loft. Abe asked Sarah when she last drank milk. She couldn't remember. And he asked her when she last ate cheese. She wasn't sure when. Abe's mouth felt thick and cottony. He didn't like the taste of milk. He wasn't much of an eater at all. But he tried to remember: When did he last drink milk? When did he last eat cheese?

Laying up in the loft that night, Abe heard his father come back. Tom told Mother he had warned neighbors. Tom said in a worried whisper that because of the dry summer the old cow had grazed far back into the woods.

Two days later, the cow died.

Tom sat the children down. "It's certain now. Our old cow had the milk fever. Cows get it in hot, dry summers. The disease doesn't stop at the cow. Somehow it poisons the cow's milk. Somehow it poisons some folks who drink the cow's milk or eat cheese made from the cow's milk."

Dennis Hanks pounded the door the next morning. He sobbed. "Mr. Sparrow woke up with a white tongue!"

Abe had never heard such fear in Dennis before.

Mother gasped, "A white coating on the tongue is the first sure sign of milk fever!" She rushed to help Mrs. Sparrow nurse Mr. Sparrow. When she came back that evening, she said grimly, "His stomach is burning—the second sure sign. He made out a will!"

Tom said, "Let us pray there is no third sign: a brown tongue."

The next day Mrs. Sparrow got a white tongue! Mr. Sparrow's tongue did turn brown, and he died. In a daze, Mrs. Sparrow realized she would likely follow her husband. Abe's mother nursed her. Sarah helped.

Abe helped his father saw planks of black cherry wood. Then Tom planed them smooth. Abe whittled pegs. The pegs would hold on the lid of the coffin. Mr. Sparrow's coffin was as fine as Tom could make it in such a short time. Tom didn't say anything, but Abe knew he started a second coffin for Mrs. Sparrow. And there were graves to dig deep into the yellow Indiana soil.

One morning when Nancy came back to the cabin, Tom asked her, "How is Mrs. Sparrow?"

Nancy winced as she sat down. "She's still alive, but not

for long. She'll be gone by afternoon or evening."

Tom said, "Rest awhile before you go back."

Abe couldn't remember seeing his mother so tired. She had been tired a lot since coming to Indiana, but today she looked old, too. She seemed far older than thirty-four.

Mother said, "I won't be going back, Tom."

Fear erupted inside Abe as if he had just heard a thousand rattlesnakes all around him.

He cried, "Mother has milk fever!"

Abe's life seemed to come to a stop. Mother was lying in bed, her face chalk white. He prayed and prayed for her life to be spared. But she got the second sign, then the third. Life no longer made any sense to Abe.

Mother was calm. She smiled at Abe and Sarah. "We will be parting soon. This is a very sad time. But we cannot always understand our heavenly Father's ways. You children won't think so, but I'm lucky. It won't be long until I see our Savior, Jesus."

Abe was nine years old when Nancy Lincoln died. He and Sarah brooded for their mother. And what if their father got milk fever?

Days after Mother was buried on a knoll in sight of the cabin, Tom took Abe and Sarah by the hand and marched them down the familiar trail to Jim Gentry's store. Then he turned and walked them down a strange trail. It took them one hour to reach a flat-roofed cabin.

Tom said, "You children must go on with your lives."

Abe heard a chorus of voices. Tom opened the door and nudged Abe and Sarah inside. Heads of children turned to gawk at them. The room fell into silence.

Tom handed a man something wrapped in cloth. Tom said, "These children are Sarah and Abe Lincoln."

And the man said, "Howdy do! I'm Andrew Crawford. Thanks kindly for the bacon. Sit down, Sarah and Abe. Take off that coonskin cap, Abe."

Tom Lincoln turned and left.

Andrew Crawford taught a blab school. But he spent the whole morning on manners. Pupils practiced saying a cheerful "howdy do!" When a boy entered a room he took off his cap. Outside, boys tipped their caps and introduced themselves. Girls curtsied. Boys and girls both practiced opening doors for older folks.

Abe ate his lunch of corn dodgers and dried apples next to a boy who was older but about Abe's size.

The boy said, "Howdy do, Abe. I'm Matt Gentry."

"Your father must run the general store."

"Yes, he does. Isn't your father the carpenter?"

Abe was stunned. He thought of his father Tom as a farmer. Matt called his father a carpenter, a man who made things out of wood. That made Abe the "carpenter's son." He had read those very words in the good book a hundred times. It took his breath away.

CHAPTER 4

Of course, Abe knew the carpenter's son Jesus was really the Son of God. Abe was only a boy. Still, he wanted to believe it was a sign from God that he might amount to something.

The next year was rough on twelve-year-old Sarah. She worked hard to do all the work her mother had done in the cabin and garden. Abe and Tom helped but weren't as particular as Sarah. And besides, they had work in the fields and forest to do.

One month before Christmas, Tom said, "Children, I have to go on a trip." And Tom rode off on a horse without a word of explanation.

Abe was only ten. He had never felt more hopeless. He acted cheerful for Sarah. Every night he prayed for his father to return.

Would they spend Christmas alone?

What if his father never came back at all?

A few days before Christmas, Abe and Sarah were inside the cabin when they heard a wagon rattling up the the trail.

"Maybe it's Father!" yelled Sarah.

"He didn't take a wagon," reasoned Abe glumly, but he ran out of the cabin with Sarah. He couldn't give up hope.

Off the wagon jumped a boy about half as tall as Abe. He stuck out his chest. "I'm John. I'm seven."

A girl stepped down. "I am Elizabeth. I am nine." She pointed at a young girl clinging to the wagon. "That is Matilda. She's five."

Abe blurted, "Are you folks just passing through?"

Suddenly Tom stood there with a woman. He said, "This is Sally, your new mother. All the way from Elizabethtown."

Abe was flabbergasted. What could he say? Before he could think of anything to say, Sally hugged him. And Abe looked into one of the kindest faces he had ever seen. She handed Abe two books he had never read before: *Robinson Crusoe* and *Arabian Nights*. So this was how God answered his prayers. Sally was a thousand times better than anything he had asked for.

Now Abe remembered his mother saying how kind the widow Sally Johnston was. Tom had certainly remembered.

Sally didn't come empty-handed. Abe helped Tom unload a chest of drawers, a table, some chairs, a box of clothing, a box of bedding, and many kitchen utensils. Tom built a second bedstead for the three girls. Abe and John would sleep in the loft.

The new family celebrated the birth of Jesus. Sally roasted a turkey Tom shot, stuffed with roots and nuts the children had gathered in the forest.

When Sally saw the bounty from Sarah's labor in the garden, she gave her a special hug. She cried, "Sarah has put up peas, turnips, beets, radishes, onions—and look at all the potatoes. What treasures!"

That was when Abe realized Sally and her children must have had a rough time, too. All the food he took for granted was treasure to them. In the Dutch oven in the fireplace, Sally baked johnnycakes made from cornmeal, water, and butter. They had syrup from sugar maples. They ate on pewter dishes. Abe felt like he was being born into something special again.

Abe wouldn't rest until something was done he had promised his real mother as she was dying. He had written Preacher Elkins in Kentucky. And when the preacher finally came to Indiana to visit a son, he went with the Lincolns to Nancy's grave. Abe was sure his mother heard Preacher Elkins's eulogy. After that, Abe didn't feel guilty for being so happy with his new mother. He was sure it was God's plan.

In the forest, Abe was handling an axe like a man. His long arms delivered such a powerful stroke, he buried the axe deeper into the wood than most men. One neighbor, hearing how fast the trees fell, thought there were several men working back in the rough. "No," said Tom, "it was only Abe." And now John helped Abe by stacking brush against trees.

Abe told story after story to John.

And John had stories to tell. He didn't have the kind of stories Abe craved, like the story that there was a new state west of Indiana called Illinois. But John had seen some mighty strange characters come and go in Elizabethtown. After all, he had lived only one block from Hardin County Courthouse. His favorite story was about the circus that had come to town. Each time he told the story, the elephant got bigger, and the lion roared louder, and the trained seal got smarter.

Abe put down his axe and sighed. "Of course, John, you know we have real bears, wolves, and panthers prowling loose right here in this forest."

John's voice was dry. "I do hear thrashing around our cabin at night." He laughed nervously. "I bet it's just the hounds."

Abe was serious. "A panther jumped the Bowers boy and girl a few years ago."

John gulped. "A panther?"

Abe said, "A panther is a hermit of an animal. It doesn't hang around roads and trails during the day." He gave John a stern look. "Just don't take any shortcuts through the forest."

"I'll remember that." John frowned, probably wondering if Abe was trying to scare him.

Abe should have let the forest speak for itself.

A huge black form appeared from out of nowhere. It seemed taller than the trees. The bear sniffed the air, smelled the sweat of boys, and thundered back into the brush.

By 1821, when Abe was twelve, the Lincolns and their neighbors had been clearing land and planting corn for five years. The area opened up just as Abe had imagined it years earlier. Once, Abe felt the Lincolns were isolated. Now, within one mile of the Lincoln cabin were seven other cabins. Abe sat down one day and scratched a mark in the yellow soil for every child in those seven cabins.

He whistled. "Forty young folks! And that doesn't include the five of us."

Church had been held for many years, but never in a special building. It was time to build a regular church building. And who was better qualified to supervise the construction than the best carpenter in the county: Tom Lincoln? So he and the neighbors built a solid church twenty-six feet by thirty feet. Tom and Sally were official members.

The children went to the church every Sunday, too. But in those days it was not the custom to make them official members. Men and women became members when they got married like Elizabeth did that same year when she married Dennis Hanks. She and Dennis lived in a cabin one mile east of the Lincolns.

Abe became a sexton in the church. He ordered supplies and kept records. As he swept the floor, he would remember the persuasion in Preacher Elkins's voice and his gestures. Every Sunday morning he listened to a sermon, too. He got in the habit of preaching a sermon himself Sunday afternoon.

If Abe was still preaching to John and Matilda on Monday, Tom would notice no one was working and say, "Abe must be on the stump again." And Tom would remind Abe and his audience the heavenly Father wished them to earn their daily bread.

Abe got the habit of taking a book with him everywhere. It was as natural as grabbing an apple. Every moment he took a break from work, he read. He treasured one new book written by Ben Franklin about himself. Franklin detailed how he improved himself by setting goals for each day, and at the end of the day reviewed how well he succeeded. Abe understood Franklin's ambition perfectly. Abe had a burning desire to improve himself. He loved the woods, but he didn't want to spend a lifetime cutting down trees. And he knew farming was not for him, as important as it was to raise food for folks to eat.

A second book thrilled him even more. It told the life of George Washington. Abe had never known of such a sense of duty—other than the saints in the Bible. Here was a man who lived only a few years before Abe was born. He was a man of action, but he showed such moral perfection that Abe was astounded. Washington would forever be Abe's ideal American. Abe couldn't hear the word "patriot" without thinking of George Washington, and the fact that Washington believed it was his duty to carry out God's plan confirmed his perfection for Abe.

In the yellow soil Abe scratched the words: "Good boys who to their books apply/Will all be great to me by and by." Abe began to think how governments worked. He began to see why man-made laws were necessary in addition to God's commandments in the Bible. The Bible didn't say exactly how folks paid for a school. It didn't say how folks should determine whether a man accused of a crime was innocent or guilty. Abe knew man-made laws fell short of being perfect. Otherwise, white folks wouldn't own black slaves. How did that happen? He burned to know. Tom told him a man named Henry Clay from Kentucky persuaded folks to accept the "Missouri Compromise." That meant the new state of Missouri would permit slaves, but no new states north of a certain line would allow slaves. When Abe talked to John about it, John just shook his head. Why talk about such complicated things? John just wanted to talk about the elephants.

Years passed. Sarah got married. Now she was a neighbor. Abe visited courtrooms whenever he could. Folks were puzzled by the gangly young giant. What would become of him? He was a sexton in the church. He could split rails faster than anyone else. He could wrestle anyone to the ground. He talked about things nobody but a lawyer or a teacher could understand. But he didn't seem cut out for doing anything in particular.

And then, once again, tragedy struck.

CHAPTER 5

Sadness overwhelmed Abe again. Sarah, the sweet girl who had been sister, brother, and mother to Abe, died giving birth to a baby. Abe wanted to lash out at something with his sinewy, axe-wielding arms—but he could do nothing but pray Sarah was with Jesus in heaven.

His friend Matt Gentry lost his mind. One moment Matt was fine. The next moment he was babbling, lost somewhere beyond reach. Abe waited for Matt to get better, but he didn't get better. It seemed to Abe as if by not being able to decide what to do in life, he was waiting around until something bad happened to him, too. Abe couldn't fritter his life away. Tom urged him to try other things.

Abe tried ferrying folks across the Ohio River. Allen Gentry offered Abe a different job. Allen was going to pilot a flatboat of corn and pork all the way to New Orleans. Abe accepted the offer. Tom had taken a flatboat to New Orleans himself—one year before Sarah was born. Maybe Abe would get married when he got back. He could hardly imagine any girl who would be interested in such a strange young man as himself.

The flatboat drifted downriver into ever warmer, wetter air. While tied to shore one night near Baton Rouge, the flatboat was attacked by thieves. Abe and Allen could have jumped into the river and saved themselves, but they refused to surrender their cargo. The thieves were shocked to see a towering fury leaping about in the moonlight—a fury who broke bones with a thunderous, whacking axe handle. The attackers fled, thankful to be alive. And Abe thanked God to be alive.

The trip to New Orleans became a bad dream to Abe. He saw slaves auctioned. He saw white men poke fingers into black people as if they were livestock. New Orleans seemed thousands of years old, with sin everywhere. He couldn't wait to get home again. But what would he do with his life when he got back home? He would turn twenty years old on the way back to Indiana on a steamboat. All the way on the Mississippi River to Cairo in Ilinois, Abe prayed. All the way up the Ohio River to Troy in Indiana, he prayed. And he noticed the boat seemed to go in every direction on the looping rivers yet stayed on a relentless course from New Orleans to Troy.

The Gentrys liked Abe. He worked in their store after he got back. It would have been hard to find a better clerk than Abe. He was a true pioneer, so he knew what folks needed. He was so strong he could lift a keg full of nails into a wagon. He could read. He knew how to work with numbers. He could keep records. He was honest.

And more than one newcomer was startled enough to blurt, "A giant!" Abe now towered six feet four inches tall and weighed over two hundred lean-muscled pounds.

Working in the store was to Abe's liking, too. It seemed like folks hadn't stopped talking politics since the national election the year before. Andrew Jackson, the great hero of the War of 1812, ran against President John Quincy Adams. Jackson, calling himself a Democrat, won the election. Abe loved to hear folks talk politics.

Abe felt he could prosper as a clerk, too. Had God answered his prayers? He still lived with his father, but that wasn't unusual for a man his age. The law even said he had to give his earnings to his father until he turned twenty-one. Not that Tom needed Abe's money. Tom Lincoln had prospered from his dozen years in Indiana. He owned one hundred hogs. He harvested many acres of corn. He started building a house for Sally that no one would call a cabin.

And then Sally's sons-in-law did something that turned the Lincolns' world upside down.

Squire Hall, the husband of Matilda, and Dennis Hanks, the husband of Elizabeth, announced they were moving west —to the state of Illinois. Sally couldn't bear being separated from her daughters. Abe suddenly discovered Tom and Sally were going to Illinois, too!

Abe went along. Of course, they moved in the winter. They traveled in two wagons. The trip was two hundred miles over frozen mud and ice-covered streams. But the long cold journey in wagons gave Abe time to think. He was grown now. It was time for him to fly from the nest. As always, he prayed that God would let him do what was right. The three families stopped in central Illinois, just west of Decatur. Once again, Tom and Abe built a cabin plus corrals and a shed for the livestock.

Abe was not happy that year of 1830. He felt more out of place than ever. He didn't even have his clerking job now. He didn't want to spend his life always clearing new land, always plowing new soil. Winter came again. And it was the kind of winter that ices the land only once in a hundred years. After a blizzard dumped deep snow, the temperature never got above zero for two months!

"Who can withstand God's icy blast?" said Abe to Tom and

Sally. The thought from Psalm 147 never seemed more true.

The winter was very hard on the newcomers because they didn't have large stores of food. But they survived. And by the time of spring thaws, everyone was anxious to get outside and work. Abe was so desperate to get some business, he was talked into piloting a flatboat of some goods to New Orleans again. On the way down to the Sangamon River, the flatboat ran aground for awhile at a village called New Salem. Months later, after Abe sold the corn and pork at New Orleans, he returned to Tom and Sally to say farewell. Then Abe headed for the village of New Salem. He was twenty-two and on his own at last.

He clerked in New Salem. He was so good at it, most folks quickly came to respect him. But New Salem was not like living on a farm. Rough men lived in villages. Jack Armstrong, the leader of the "Clary Grove gang," challenged the newcomer to wrestle. But Armstrong was no match for a giant who had labored in the farm and forest almost every waking hour of his life.

Jack Armstrong was a good loser. Abe was nothing like the roughnecks Jack knew. Abe didn't drink alcohol. He didn't smoke tobacco. But Abe did know how to poke fun at himself. He did tell jokes. He did have a story for every situation. He never lied. And he was a wizard at figuring things out—practical things, too. Abe made a friend for life in Jack Armstrong.

New Salem was different from the farm in another way, too. Men met to debate each other. They called themselves "freethinkers," and Abe quickly found they thought they were free to think and say anything. Abe was shocked. It was the first time he had ever heard men question out loud whether

Jesus was God. They wondered if Adam really did sin—and, if he did sin, did Jesus really pay for that sin? They wondered why if God was good, He would allow death and pain in the world. They questioned everything.

It wasn't as if Abe hadn't asked these questions. He had. Before he could read, the true answers to his questions came from his mother's lips. And after he could read, he found the true answers himself in the Bible. Abe realized that, as much as he hated their attitude about Jesus, he had asked similar questions. So, if he denied these freethinkers the right to speak out, he would be a hypocrite.

Maybe he could change some of their minds. He could not have done that to men who kept their doubts secret and pretended to believe in Jesus. Some of the men snickered at Abe. Did this backwoods roughneck who just whipped Jack Armstrong in the dusty street think he could debate educated men like a schoolmaster and a doctor?

But Abe knew the Bible by heart, and he could remember verses to advance his arguments. He especially liked to make the point that the souls of all folks could be saved. No one was picked ahead of time to go to hell. He believed God had a plan for everyone, but folks still had to make their own choices to be saved.

He raised his arms toward the ceiling and quoted Saint Paul in 1 Corinthians 15:22. "For as in Adam all die, even so in Christ shall all be made alive."

The freethinkers argued with Abe. And Abe countered their arguments with reasoned arguments from the Bible. Their challenge was actually strengthening his spiritual armor. After awhile, Abe could tell the men were amazed a roughneck like

Abe had such power to reason and persuade. He worried about being too proud of himself. After all, he had God's Word to help him.

After one debate the doctor admitted, "You know, Abe, I really do believe Jesus is God."

Abe was surprised. "Why, you just argued hot and heavy in a debate that there is no God at all."

The doctor said, "I just like to take different sides in a debate. It helps me think things out better."

Abe replied, "I see debating is a powerful way of turning a subject inside and out." The truth was that Abe had always done that. He debated within himself.

The doctor said, "Abe, you're very good at speaking, but you still need more practice."

"Practice for what?" Abe sensed something very big was happening to him.

CHAPTER 6

The doctor put his hand up on Abe's shoulder.

"Abe," he said, "folks, educated and uneducated, want a righteous, God-fearing man to represent their needs in the state legislature—the group of men who make the laws of Illinois. The people decide which man that is going to be with their votes. So a man has to know how to speak to them. A man has to convince them that he is the right man. And I think you might be that right man, Abe."

Abe was astounded. "Do you want me to run for the legislature?"

"Yes, I do, Abe."

The legislature? Abe, a man of the people? Abe mumbled, "It can't hurt me too much to try."

The doctor said, "Abe, you have more than the skill to debate. You have the courage of a believer who knows he is serving God by serving men and women."

The more Abe thought about it, the more eager he got. It was almost too good to be true. He hadn't lived in New Salem one year yet, and he was going to run for the Illinois legislature. Maybe he would amount to something.

He thought of a plan to get elected, too.

He practiced his speech in the store. "Friends, I know a thing or two about rivers." He tucked his thumbs under imaginary suspenders. "I've been busy boating over the Sangamon River, measuring depths and plotting them on maps I made. New Salem has a great future for river commerce. I want you to vote for me because I can offer you something that the other candidates can't offer you—a plan for prosperity." Abe raised his hands to the ceiling and went up on his toes.

Jack Armstrong rushed in. "Come on, Abe. A rider is here with a message from the governor!"

"What is going on?" Abe loped out the door. He found himself out in the street with dozens of other men.

The rider shouted, "Chief Black Hawk is on the warpath! Up in northern Illinois. We need men to fight!"

Fight! War! Abe couldn't believe his ears. He had never seen an Indian who was really living in the wild like a Indian. Tom told him how his father—Abe's Grandpappy Abraham —was shot dead by an Indian right in front of Tom. Uncle Mord told the same story. But it didn't seem real to Abe. Besides, Abe knew Indians had been cheated by white men. Maybe as much as black folks.

Abe argued with himself. Indians had been wronged. But could he stand by doing nothing while innocent settlers were killed? And he knew some white men who hated Indians. What if only that kind of white man volunteered to fight? Indian women and children might be murdered.

Abe volunteered.

He had to borrow a horse. He rode hard to join sixty men gathered at a village called Richland. There was a real army officer there standing behind stacks of muskets. The officer barked, "Who is your captain?"

Jack Armstrong yelled, "I intend to come back alive. I want Abe Lincoln for a captain. Abe can whip anybody."

Abe was stunned. How could he lead men into war? He was

relieved when another man yelled, "I want Bill Kirkpatrick for captain!"

Men surged toward Abe and Kirkpatrick. Three times as many men surrounded Abe. "That settles it," cried the army officer. "Abe Lincoln here is captain of this company of mounted volunteers. Get your muskets and ride north, men."

Abe had never been so proud. He had been "elected" leader of the sixty men. He remembered the Bible. Pride was dangerous. He kept that thought in his head as the company rode north to find Black Hawk.

Abe never even saw Chief Black Hawk. But he learned about brave men who volunteered for such hardship. He learned what an officer has to do to keep order. His company seemed always one camp away from the fight. He knew that because they arrived the next day to bury the dead. The sight of the dead men haunted him.

Abe reenlisted twice anyway. Once he saved the life of a friendly Indian who was about to be killed by some soldiers.

When the war was over, Abe felt like he had served with honor. He had been called to duty, and he went. He didn't have to shoot another man. He accepted that fate as God's plan.

He returned to New Salem three weeks before the election. He found out his job as clerk was gone. The man who owned the store was gone, too. Abe didn't have time to worry. He campaigned hard. He showed his charts of the Sangamon River and rattled off figures. He lost.

The doctor said, "Don't be bitter, Abe."

Abe wasn't bitter. He figured God didn't think he was ready to be a lawmaker in the legislature. He knew the voters didn't think he was ready. Abe studied law all the harder.

But he had to earn a living, too. He didn't have his clerk's job.

A man offered him a chance to be his partner in a general store. Abe jumped at the chance. He used the $125 he received for his service in the Mounted Volunteers. But Abe's partner was reckless. The business borrowed more and more money. Finally, no one would loan them more money. The store closed. Abe had debts to pay off. He had failed at business. He was only twenty-three and deep in debt.

He still had a good reputation. For the next two years, he earned his living any way he could. He taught himself how to survey and earned money that way. He worked as the postmaster. He clerked in several stores. He wrote simple contracts for folks. He never lost his sense of humor, and he never lost the conviction that God had a plan for him.

Abe was a fearless storyteller around other men. But he drew inside his shell around women. He felt more than ever he was too uneducated, too uncultured, too awkward, and too ugly. He was twenty-five years old now. He wanted a wife, but he couldn't act natural around women. He froze up. He liked Ann Rutledge enough to actually approach her and speak to her. But he learned her heart belonged to another man, even though that man had gone away from New Salem. Ann said she would never give up hope.

In two short years, Abe had failed as a politician and a businessman. Would he also fail ever to win a woman's heart? Abe knew the Bible. The saints failed, too—many times. Suffering made a man stronger.

So he ran for the Illinois legislature again.

He called himself a Whig this time, because Henry Clay of Kentucky was a Whig. Tom Lincoln told Abe years before that Henry Clay was a man to admire: Clay was against slavery. Clay was for a strong nation. Abe liked Clay, too. Abe was more relaxed running for election this time. He failed once. And he would probably fail this time, too. So he told jokes. He had no elaborate plan for the Sangamon River.

And he won the election.

"Abe," said the doctor, "you won the election because folks know you will do what is right."

In no time at all, Abe found himself among eight hundred people living in Vandalia, the state capital of Illinois. Again he threw himself into a new situation, nervous about being unprepared and unworthy. He bought his first suit. But he still felt like a gawky, shaggy colt in the midst of prancing, shiny thoroughbreds.

John Stuart had just been elected for the second time. John liked the modest giant from New Salem who could tell stories. He took Abe around Vandalia with him. That was wonderful for Abe, who felt so unsure of himself in fine company. Stuart knew exactly how to act in every social situation. Abe studied his every move and learned fast. And he learned something else. Many of the lawyers in the state capital had taught themselves law and passed the examination to get a law license. Now Abe knew he had been right in studying law by himself. He studied law all the harder.

Within two years, Abe passed the law examination. He was a real lawyer. As if to remind Abe life is fragile and unpredictable, Ann Rutledge got a fever and died. She never married.

Abe was reelected. Illinois moved its state capital to Springfield. Abe roomed there with merchant Josh Speed, who soon became his close friend. Abe opened a law office with John Stuart. He got reelected again in 1838. He was successful in every way but two. He still owed money in New Salem. And he wanted a wife—even if the Bible did assure him it was no disgrace not to have a wife. He prayed for God's will to be done.

At a party in December 1839, John Stuart introduced Abe to his cousin Mary Todd. She was all the things Abe feared most in a woman. She was so tiny he gawked down at the part of her fawn brown hair. He felt like Goliath. She had a turned-up nose and a sharp chin. She was very pretty. He felt uglier than ever. She was perky. Her ivory skin flushed pink as she laughed. He felt like a slow, lumbering bear. She was from a very rich family in Kentucky. Could he ever tell such a lady he grew up in a crowded one-room cabin?

She smiled. "I'm a Whig, too, Mr. Lincoln."

Abe couldn't believe such a pretty lady knew politics at all, but he would be polite. "Why is that, Miss Todd?"

"Why, I've been a Whig ever since I met Henry Clay."

"Henry Clay!" He was amazed.

"Mr. Clay is a friend of my father's." Mary Todd gave Abe a look that pierced his heart like an arrow. There was no mistaking what her look meant!

CHAPTER 7

Mary Todd actually liked him!

Abe thought he might actually like her, too. As Mary brightly talked politics, which Abe loved, she became more and more precious in his eyes. Yes, he liked her very much.

They were so unlike each other. And yet they seemed meant for each other. They saw each other often. They became engaged to be married. Marriage would have been soon if Mary's sister hadn't opposed it. Her sister's objections were so true that they hurt Abe. He was ten years older than Mary. Worst of all, he still owed money. He couldn't buy Mary the fine things she was used to having.

Abe crumbled under his doubts. He broke off the engagement. He slipped into a deep depression some folks called the "blues."

He asked God, "How could I ever be good enough for such a fine lady?"

Abe was soon to learn God's plans for us can be very complicated. Abe's friend, Josh Speed, who had moved to Kentucky, was going through the same doubts before he married his sweetheart, Fanny. Abe visited him. Abe could counsel someone else's fears with cool, calm logic.

Josh's mother knew Abe was having problems, too. She gave Abe a beautiful white Bible. "This really is the best cure for your blues, Abe."

By the time the visit was over, Josh was cured. Abe confessed to Josh, "I believe God made me an instrument of bringing Fanny and you together. . . ."

He didn't tell Josh he was cured of the blues, too, because he wasn't sure he could make things right with Mary. He humiliated her when he broke the engagement.

He visited Mary to ask for forgiveness. Mary was wonderful about it. They agreed to stay friends. Mary wrote letters to a newspaper poking fun at one of Abe's political rivals. Politics in those days could erupt into more than a battle of words —Abe's friend John Stuart and Stephen Douglas debated each other once with their fists.

Abe's political rival erupted, too. After he saw the letters in the newspaper, he challenged Abe to a duel. Abe could have said Mary wrote the letters, but he took the blame. He figured he couldn't talk his way out of a duel with an apology. He couldn't. It seemed like a bad dream.

Abe got to pick the place and the weapons. He sent details to his rival. They would meet in the woods along the Mississippi River near St. Louis. Each would fight with the kind of long flat sword used by soldiers in the cavalry. The two duelists had to stay always within a rectangle ten feet by twelve feet. Abe's friends thought his choice of weapons was a joke meant to make his rival see how foolish they were both acting.

His rival didn't think it was a joke. He showed up with two swords at the edge of the great river. Abe arrived, too. Friends of both duelists managed to talk Abe's rival out of dueling only at the last second.

If any of Abe's friends had ever seen him swing an axe they would have known he wasn't joking about using swords. Not one man in a thousand could withstand one of Abe's colossal strokes. He would have split the man like a pine log.

Abe shuddered to think what might have happened. He was so ashamed that he would never talk about it again. He promised God he would grin and walk away from a fight the rest of his life—even if he didn't feel like grinning.

Mary was thrilled. She didn't know Abe was ashamed. He hid it. She thought Abe was very brave to protect her. That bizarre incident brought them back together.

Abe and Mary married in November 1842. Etched inside Mary's wedding band were the words: "Love is Eternal."

The next years were busy, look-straight-ahead years of an ambitious man's life. Abe continued to build his political reputation. But he didn't run for legislature again. He had to get out of debt. He "rode the circuit," which meant he was a lawyer who rode out to take cases from folks in villages and rural areas. He was gone six months out of the year. But it was the surest, honest way Abe knew to make money fast.

The first years were very difficult for Mary. Her sister had been right. The Mary who once wore the fanciest clothes could now afford nothing fancy. The Mary who once lived in a mansion now lived above a tavern. A son, Bobby, was born. He was a rowdy boy. When Abe came back from the circuit, he would comfort Mary. Then he would have to go out and work harder.

Finally, there was light at the end of the tunnel. Abe was completely out of debt. They bought a fine, white two-story frame house in downtown Springfield. Abe was very proud of Mary. She had endured the hardship. Bobby and their next son, Eddie, had a nice fenced-in yard to play in.

Abe took young lawyer Billy Herndon into his law practice. Abe was setting the stage for a new phase of his career.

He was planning to run for the U.S. House of Representatives the next year. That meant he and Mary would have to live in Washington, D.C. That meant Billy Herndon had to keep their law practice alive until Abe got back to Springfield.

Mary didn't think much of Abe's new partner. Billy was cocky. He was a chatterbox who thought he could figure everybody out. He was wild, too, preferring the tavern to church. He griped about some of Abe's habits. His complaints got back to Mary. Billy didn't like the way Abe came in and read newspapers out loud every morning. Billy didn't like the way Bobby and Eddie came in and roughhoused in their law office.

Abe knew all of that about Billy, too. But he knew something else. Billy was completely loyal to him. Maybe Billy complained, but no one else could complain about Abe in front of Billy. Billy would challenge him on the spot.

Abe forgave Billy's faults. And Billy forgave Abe his faults. They loved each other like brothers. Abe knew he would be leaving his law practice in faithful hands if he won the election.

He won the election. Abe and his family left for Washington, D.C., in January 1848. About half of the 227 members of the House of Representatives belonged to the Democrat political party. The other half belonged to the Whig Party. The president was Democrat James Polk. Polk had waged war against Mexico for two years. Some Whigs like Abe thought this was really a war to get more land and extend slavery—because the Missouri Compromise arranged by Henry Clay allowed new states to the south to have slavery. Of course, at the time of the compromise, Henry Clay didn't think there would ever be any new states to the south. The war with Mexico would change all that.

Abe took a strong stand against the war. He expected the other Whigs to back him up. But they didn't.

One Whig told him, "Why make the slavery people mad? Let's just hope nothing bad happens."

Abe had spoken out against slavery before. Now he was going to do something about it. He was going to introduce a bill that would phase out slavery in Washington, D.C. if Congress would vote in favor of his bill. He figured that would be a small start toward solving a monstrous problem.

Another Whig found out his plan. He asked Abe, "Have you lost your senses? Don't you know that bill will make the slavery people furious?"

Abe was disappointed in his fellow Whigs once again, but he campaigned hard for Zachary Taylor, the Whig candidate for president in the 1848 election. Abe was meeting other powerful people in the Whig Party, too. They found out how capable he was, but after Taylor won the election, Abe found out what they really thought of him. After every presidential election, the new president appointed hundreds of people to judgeships, commissions, and other government agencies. Abe gave the new president, Taylor, a modest list of qualified people from Illinois. Not one person on his list was appointed.

Abe soon found out President Taylor and other Whig leaders thought he was too pushy. He was too outspoken. Why irritate the Democrats and slave owners? There could be a war between the free states and slave states. No one wanted war.

The leading Whigs had lots of experience. Abe thought

it over long and hard. His final conclusion made his blood run cold: Unless reasonable people solved the slavery problem, soon there would be a war anyway. The entire United States, such a promising young nation founded on such wonderful ideals of freedom, might go up in flames. He was overwhelmed with sadness.

What was Abe supposed to do? The others in his own Whig political party refused to listen to him. He prayed for God's help.

After that, for some reason he could think of nothing but Mary. Her father had recently died. She had gone home to Kentucky for awhile. She had to force herself to return. She didn't like Washington, D.C. She thought the people were snobs. In spite of her own rich family, Mary had never been a snob. What other rich young lady would have openly embraced a rough country lawyer like Abe Lincoln?

Abe's heart ached. Mary had endured hardship for him and the boys. Just when they moved into a nice home in Springfield and Mary was her bubbly self again, Abe yanked her away from it. Now his sweet little Mary was unhappy again. God must be telling him to fix that.

One evening after they put the boys to bed, Abe said, "Mary, we need to make a powerful big decision."

CHAPTER 8

Abe put his huge paw over Mary's tiny hand. "I'm thinking of getting out of politics."

"Are you sure you want to do that?" Her voice betrayed how happy she was to hear that news.

"Why don't we go back to Springfield after my term is over?"

Mary perked up. "Maybe little Eddie would get better. He's been so sick here in Washington, D.C."

And they did return to Springfield. Abe plunged into his law practice with his loyal partner Billy Herndon. Mary loved her big house. But their joy was short-lived. Eddie, not yet four years old, died. Mary sunk into the depths of despair. She was touched to see a poem in the local newspaper entitled "Little Eddie."

And the angel of death was hovering up high
And the lovely boy was called to die
Bright is the home to him now given
For such is the kingdom of heaven.

The newspaper didn't reveal who wrote the poem, but Mary knew who wrote it. Abe wrote it. He was sure Eddie was in heaven. He had to make sure Mary knew it, too.

Mary began to feel better. When Mary found out she was going to have another baby, both she and Abe were sure the baby was God's gift.

Willie was born in December 1850. About the same time, Abe found out that his father Tom was deathly sick. Abe had drifted apart from his father. He couldn't resolve whatever difference he had with his father, and he wouldn't talk about it. That's the way Abe was with a problem he couldn't solve. He didn't complain. He didn't gossip. He did what the Bible said; he prayed and he hoped.

He wrote his stepbrother John and urged him to tell his father Tom to trust "our great, and good, and merciful maker" and "if it is to be his lot to go now, he will soon have a joyous meeting with many loved ones gone before. . . ."

One month later, Abe's father, Tom, died.

Death seemed to pull Abe closer to God. More and more of his loved ones were in God's paradise. Abe accepted God's dominion with all his heart and mind.

He told a preacher at the time, "I examine the issues of life and death as rigorously as I examine any issue in a courtroom. I always conclude that divine authority and inspiration of the Bible are absolute certainties."

The next years were golden. In 1853, baby Tom was born. He wiggled like a little tadpole. Abe always called him Tad. Bobby was now almost ten, and Willie was three. The house was noisy. The boys were healthy. Mary was happy.

Abe practiced law, which he loved. His image as a skilled lawyer with a great sense of humor was set in these happy, relaxed years. Abe had thousands of stories he could tell to make a point. Some were funny, and some were not. He didn't make up stories. He collected them. He was a masterful storyteller who never seemed to forget even one line of a story after he heard it.

He had the Bible memorized, too. It was due to his habit of always reading aloud. He felt by using the two senses of hearing and seeing instead of just one sense of seeing, he could remember almost anything he read. He could quote by heart all the Psalms, entire chapters of Isaiah, and almost all of the New Testament. He used verses from the Bible to make points, too. And his favorite method of persuasion he learned from the Bible. Abe knew Jesus told parables because most folks remembered entertaining stories much longer than they remembered preaching.

Abe might have spent the rest of his life practicing law in Springfield if he hadn't read one morning in his newspaper about Stephen Douglas running for reelection to the U.S. Senate in 1858.

"Billy!" Abe turned a stunned face to his law partner. "It says here Douglas wants every state to vote whether it wants slavery! Even the states where black people are now free!" Abe groaned. "The problem of slavery just won't go away. It's going to get worse!"

Billy sighed. "You're the only man in Illinois who can beat Stephen Douglas."

"I don't want to go back to Washington, D.C. . . ." Abe paused. "But what choice do I have now?"

The race for the position of Illinois senator wouldn't have attracted much attention in earlier years. But Douglas had become a national figure. He had personally destroyed the "Missouri Compromise" in 1854 when he devilishly pushed through a change in the law that allowed any state to adopt slavery. He was the man who spoke of slavery. He was a powerful speaker, too, so gifted he could make decent folks think slavery was all right. There was only one way to prevent that.

Abe said to Bill, "I'll debate him."

"That rascal is too smart to debate you."

The old Whig Party had disintegrated over slavery. A new political party called the Republican Party formed against slavery. At their convention, Abe gave a speech that used the Savior's own words, "A house divided against itself cannot stand." Abe added, "I believe this government cannot endure, permanently half slave and half free."

His speech was published in newspapers all over Illinois and even in New York. Some editors were so impressed they published the entire speech as a small book.

When Douglas heard this new Republican Party nominated Abe Lincoln as their candidate for the Senate seat from Illinois, he muttered, "I'll have my hands full now. Abe is the best stump speaker in the West."

Only Mary Todd Lincoln was unhappier than Douglas. But Mary knew politics. She knew this race was much bigger than just a Senate race. It was slavery against freedom. It might make Abe a national figure.

Abe showed up at the first rally for Douglas. Douglas was amused. He even invited Abe up on the platform. Abe spoke to the same crowd the next day. Abe destroyed everything Douglas had said.

At the next rally for Douglas, Abe was there again. The next day he gave his speech, ripping apart Douglas's speech. Douglas was no longer amused.

Abe kept following Douglas around Illinois, blasting apart his opponent's speeches. Newspaper reporters soon realized that both he and Douglas were magnificent speakers. The New York newspapers said, "Illinois is the most interesting political battleground in the United States."

Douglas finally realized Abe had outsmarted him. By always speaking last, Abe was hammering the last nail in every time. What could he do about it?

Abe offered a suggestion, "Debate me on the same day."

And Douglas was trapped.

They agreed to travel around the state to have a total of seven debates. Mary was thrilled now. She wished Abe good luck and blurted, "Now I know you'll be president someday, Abe."

"President!" Abe was amazed. He could only laugh.

Abe prayed for God's help. He would speak the truth during the debates, whether that was politically smart or not. He would urge folks to honor the Declaration of Independence: All men are created equal.

Douglas created fear. Did folks want blacks flooding into Illinois? Did they want blacks marrying their daughters? Did they want blacks riding in the same carriages? Eating in the same inns? In spite of Douglas's treachery, Abe got 190,000 votes and Douglas got 176,000 votes. But the senator wasn't elected by popular vote. The newly elected Illinois state representatives voted for a senator. And Democrats outnumbered Republicans fifty-four to forty-six.

Abe lost the election!

But both men now were national figures. Both were seen —even in the East—as the best spokesmen their political parties had to offer. Two years later, these two men got the nominations from their parties to run for president. But to show

how divided the country was over slavery, two more political parties formed. Four men would be on the ballot for president.

It was the same debate all over again. Abe campaigned hard for president and made his position as plain and honest as he could. He was like Henry Clay. He hated slavery and would not allow any states to leave the Union!

On election day, Abe hung around the telegraph office in Springfield to hear some early results. He was winning the popular vote for president. But he had won the popular vote before. Would he lose once again because the rules were strange? Each state was allotted a certain number of "electoral votes," according to how many people lived in that state. But the winner of the popular vote in that state got all the electoral votes whether he won the popular vote by one vote or one hundred thousand votes! So, even in the national election, it was possible to win the popular vote and lose the election anyway.

Abe walked back to wait with Mary at their home. In 1860, it took a very long time to total up all the votes around the nation.

Abe thanked God for his chance. How many men got to run for president? Now he would just have to wait and see God's plan.

Would God decide Abe should fail again?

Mary said, "You should grow a beard, Abe."

"Why? I've never had a beard my whole life. I'm fifty-one years old, Mary."

She smiled. "A beard will make the new president look so dignified."

Abe laughed. "I will grow a beard. God knows I need all

the help I can get." Abe could always laugh at himself. When some folks called him a gorilla, Abe just laughed and said, "I'm a bit smarter, I hope."

There was a knock on the door. The minute they saw Billy Herndon's face, Abe and Mary knew the result. . . .

A smile almost split Billy's face into two halves. He yelled, "Howdy do, Mr. President!"

Giant Abe and tiny Mary danced a jig. The three boys whooped and hollered. Mary was even cordial to Billy Herndon. Abe fell into deep silence. The days ahead would be very dangerous. The slave states knew Abe was going to be very tough on slavery. They might strike quickly.

In early 1861, Abe stood on the platform at the back of a passenger train, saying farewell to his good friends of Springfield. His words were very sad. "I now leave, not knowing when or whether ever I may return, with a task before me greater than that which rested upon George Washington. Without the assistance of that Divine Being who ever attended him, I cannot succeed. With that assistance, I cannot fail."

That summed it up completely. God would decide.

All over the nation, men were drifting apart, silently taking sides. The slave states attracted many good men—men Abe knew. These men chose to defend their land and their families. Abe was very saddened by that. In making that choice, they were defending a terrible evil.

Abe was sworn in as president on March 4, 1861. He hardly had time to help Mary and the three boys get settled in the White House, the mansion for the president and his family in Washington, D.C. The slave states struck quickly. Calling themselves the Confederacy, their army attacked the United States Army at Fort Sumter in South Carolina on

April 12. The war had begun!

Two days later, Fort Sumter surrendered to the Confederates. Abe's heart ached when he got the reports of how many men had been killed. He mourned the men on both sides. This was a terrible national problem that men like himself had failed to solve. Now young men were solving the problem with their blood.

The tone of the war soon became obvious. Abe's United States Army, now called the Union Army, had vastly superior resources and numbers of men. The Union generals were timid. Abe felt like King Saul. South of Washington, D.C., there was Goliath in the person of brilliant General Robert E. Lee, standing out in the open every day, laughing and taunting the Union Army. Where was Abe's David?

In July, Abe proclaimed a national day of fasting and repenting of sins. He said, "It is fit and becoming in all people, at all times, to acknowledge and revere the Supreme government of God. . .to confess and deplore their sins and transgressions in the full conviction that the fear of the Lord is the beginning of wisdom."

Cynical politicians were stunned. Who was this new president in the White House?

Abe waited and waited for a Union victory. People of the Union became upset with him. Why couldn't the Union Army fight? One of Abe's own advisors grumbled sarcastically, "Our Union Army is dug in and watching the enemy as fast as it can."

Influential people began to tell Abe to give up and let the Confederacy go its own way. The Confederacy was perfectly willing to have a standoff. Lee and his generals were brilliant at defense. If the Confederates held out long enough, all the people in the Union might finally say, "Stop. That's enough."

Abe was heard to say, "I am a humble instrument in the hands of our heavenly Father. He permits the war to go on for some wise purpose of His own, mysterious and unknown to us. . . ." Again, the cynics shook their heads.

Suddenly, Abe and Mary's son Willie died. Mary became bedridden because she was grieving so hard. Abe prayed hard. He felt like only his faith kept him from losing his mind. How much suffering could he and Mary bear?

Word drifted in of some small Union victories along the Mississippi River. A general named Ulysses Grant seemed to be responsible.

"What kind of general is this Ulysses Grant?" asked Abe.

His advisors shrugged. "He wasn't even in the army when the war started. He has the reputation of being unreliable."

That was a polite way of saying Grant drank too much alcohol. Abe thought about it. He despised the effects of too much alcohol. But he considered alcoholics sick people, not evil people. Besides, people could change. Maybe Grant didn't have a drinking problem anymore. He would wait to see if this unreliable General Grant had any more success.

Grant did have more success. His Union Army was moving down the Mississippi, winning battle after battle. Grant was cutting the Confederacy in two!

Abe thanked God. He issued a proclamation of thanksgiving: "It is right to recognize and confess the presence of the Almighty Father. . .invoke the influence of His Holy Spirit to subdue the anger, which has produced and so long sustained a needless and cruel rebellion. . . ."

Wise people in the Union began to understand Abe. God was the master of history. Abe was His instrument. Never had an American politician stated it so plainly.

There were really two wars now. The war in the West was being won by the Union Army under Grant's relentless offensive tactics. The war in the East was being won by the Confederacy under Lee's clever defensive tactics.

Suddenly, General Lee was no longer on the defensive. He moved his Confederate Army north into the Union state of Pennsylvania. Abe tried to think like Lee. What was he doing? Lee must think the Confederacy was in trouble. Grant was capturing the West. If Lee could now lead the Confederates north right smack into the Union and win a big battle in the East, the Union might lose heart. Abe had to admit Lee was brilliant.

In a meeting with his closest advisors, Abe said, "We are not doing enough. God will help our Union Army drive Lee out of Pennsylvania, and we will declare the slaves in the rebellious states to be free." His advisors were stunned. Some said that was a terrible mistake.

But Abe prepared his Emancipation Proclamation. On September 22, 1862, he proclaimed that on the upcoming New Year's Day the slaves of the rebellious states were to be set free. On January 1, 1863, the president's proclamation took effect.

In July, Lee struck at Gettysburg in Pennsylvania. It was a bloody battle. Commanders used tactics from the old musket days. But their soldiers were armed with modern rifles. The slaughter was horrible. The Union prevailed. Lee retreated back to the slave states. Almost the same day, Grant won another great battle. He captured Vicksburg, a fortress along the Mississippi River, long considered impossible to conquer. The Union controlled the West!

In November, Abe appeared at the Gettysburg battlefield with a speech of a mere 268 words. He began, "Fourscore and seven years ago our fathers brought forth on this continent, a new nation conceived in liberty. . ." And he concluded with, "We here highly resolve that these dead shall not have died in vain; that this nation, under God, shall have new birth of freedom; and that government of the people, by the people, for the people, shall not perish from the earth."

Abe knew the Bible by heart. He knew sinful nations did perish. Some newspapers thought his speech was trivial because it was so short. But several recognized it as a masterpiece.

Back in Washington, D.C., Abe got a mild disease similar to chicken pox. He joked, "At last, I have something I can give everyone."

Abe rarely lost his sense of humor, even through those terrible days. Humor helped him cope with the constant heartbreak of war. More than one person observed Abe was the saddest-looking man they had ever seen—until they heard him joke. Then a smile transformed his face into radiant joy.

But in the beginning of 1864, the war in the East was once again bogged down. Abe simply had no general in the East who could fight. He prayed. The answer was obvious. Like Saul, Abe had his David. Abe must let him fight.

He said to his advisors, "I don't care what people say about Grant. The man fights."

He put Grant in charge of the entire Union Army—the most awesome military force ever assembled by mankind—over two hundred thousand men armed to the teeth with modern rifles and heavy artillery pieces.

The outcome seemed inevitable. But Abe was not jubilant. He knew what this meant. The two great generals of war now opposed each other in the East. Losses on both sides would be staggering. It was heartbreaking to think about how terrible it would be.

And suddenly the outcome was not inevitable at all. Abe had to get reelected president in 1864.

The two armies were deadlocked, slaughtering each other. The people of the Union were sick of the war and the bloodbath. The man running against Abe was none other than McClellan, one of the Union generals in the East Abe had fired—a very weak, indecisive man who couldn't fight.

McClellan confirmed it. He said if he were president, he would stop the war right away—the Confederacy could come back into the Union and keep their slaves!

Abe found out men in his own Republican Party were plotting to find a Republican candidate other than Abe. They didn't think Abe had a chance of being reelected.

Never in his worst dreams did Abe think the whole struggle might end up resolving nothing. He went down on his knees. Surely God would not let this happen now.

Chapter 10

Abe's great struggle to free the slaves seemed doomed. Abe knew God was never wrong. What was happening?

He prayed so many times, "Oh, please, God, give me the wisdom to know what You want me to do." Had Abe made a mistake? Had he not understood God's wishes?

He just had to continue to do what he thought was right. He began to plan how he might persuade the new President McClellan to carry through with the struggle.

Mary asked, "How can you even talk to that weakling? He failed you time and time again."

"I have no time for quarrels. There's too much to do."

But in his heart Abe knew Mary was right. McClellan would fail. He had failed Abe before—again and again.

If only Grant could defeat Lee soon. But it wasn't likely. Lee seemed determined to fight to the last man. After all, Lee knew McClellan was the answer to the Confederacy's prayers.

Abe prayed too. It was September 1864.

Eleven-year-old Tad burst into Abe's office. "General Sherman has taken Atlanta!"

Far away from the Grant-Lee struggle in the East, the Union general Sherman had captured the great rail center of the Confederacy in the South. It was an awful blow to the Confederacy.

There was hope for the Union yet. Now if only Grant's army could finish off Lee's army. But Lee's army fought on doggedly. Lee knew exactly what was at stake: If Lincoln was not reelected, McClellan would let the slave states keep their slaves—the Confederacy would win after all!

The presidential election in early November crept closer and closer. It was now the middle of October.

Abe stared at his office door. *If only dear little Tad would fling that door open again and hop in with good news. Oh, please, God. . .*

The door flung open!

Tad yelled, "General Sheridan has routed Jubal Early. We've captured the Shenandoah Valley!"

Once again, the Union had scored a giant success away from the long bloody battle between Grant and Lee. The Shenandoah Valley in Virginia was vital to the Confederacy. Its fertile soil was a major source of their food.

"Thank God," said Abe. It was all Abe needed to say.

The people of the Union now saw an end to the struggle. They had believed in Abe back in 1860. They sometimes lost faith in Abe. But now in 1864 they believed him again.

The election results trickled in.

Abe remembered the election four years earlier. So much had happened since then. He truly felt he had become an instrument of God. And he was at peace while he waited. He had done what he thought God wanted. He hadn't been lazy about it as if God would just give him the answers. He had devoted his entire heart and soul to winning the war.

Abe won 55 percent of the popular vote and won almost all the electoral votes. Once again, Abe was elected president of the United States.

The struggle to free the slaves and preserve the Union was as good as done. The presidency remained in Abe's giant hands. And Abe was in God's cosmic hands.

Abe was very tired. The fatigue seemed to settle in now and weigh him down. Abe almost seemed to shrink. If he had been a young man, he would have bounced up and looked toward his next struggle, but he knew this struggle was his last one.

Abe was sworn in as president a second time. In a speech full of quotes from the Bible, he said, "The judgments of the Lord are true and righteous all together. With malice toward none; with charity for all; with firmness in the right, as God gives us to see the right, let us strive on to finish the work we are in. . . ."

In early April of 1865, Abe had a dream. He told Mary and some close friends about it. He dreamed he heard sobbing. He began wandering through the White House. He saw soldiers guarding a coffin. Abe asked a soldier, "Who is the dead man in that coffin?" The soldier answered "Sir, it's the president. He was murdered by a crazy man."

"Oh, no!" gasped Mary.

Mary and their close friends were very sad. Abe seemed genuinely in touch with God. They knew men in the Bible got dreams from angels. Could Abe's dream become true?

But the dream was forgotten. Because on April 9, 1865, Abe got a telegram. Lee had surrendered to Grant. The war was over.

People celebrated wildly throughout the Union. Even people in the Confederacy were glad the war was over. They had suffered tremendously. And now they were thankful the terms of peace would be in the hands of a kind giant like Abe.

It was time to relax. On April 14, Abe took Mary to the Ford Theater in Washington, D.C., to watch a play. One of the actors was a twenty-seven-year-old, weak man, too cowardly to have fought in the great struggle. He was crazy, too. He wanted to take revenge for the Confederacy. He was too crazy to know that what he wanted to do would cause his own Confederacy untold suffering.

John Wilkes Booth sneaked up behind Abe and shot him in the head. Furious Union soldiers finally trapped the murderer days later, hiding like a rat in a barn, and shot him to death. Abe would not have approved of the soldiers shooting his murderer without a trial. But Abe was dead.

Abe Lincoln died the morning of April 15, 1865.

The Union mourned the loss of their great leader. Wise people in the Confederacy mourned his loss, too. When General Sherman told a Confederate general that Abe was dead, the blood drained from the Confederate general's face. He said, "The Confederacy lost the best friend we had."

The world mourned his loss, too. The great Russian writer Tolstoy said Abe's moral power and strength of character made him the greatest figure in world history since Bible times.

HARRIET TUBMAN

"MOSES" OF HER PEOPLE

by Callie Smith Grant

Inside a slave cabin on the eastern shore of the state of Maryland, an old woman sat in a rocking chair and stared into the fire crackling in her small fireplace. She remembered tending it carefully only a few hours earlier as she cooked a huge Christmas dinner for her grown children.

This was the time of year when slaves had a few days off from the work that consumed their bodies and crushed their spirits. She was sure most of her children would come home from the nearby plantations where they worked and spend the holiday with their parents. That's how they had celebrated Christmas for years, so why should 1854 be any different?

She'd killed and roasted a pig and cooked up her children's favorite foods. Then she'd waited all day for them. Even her husband had taken to looking out the door from time to time.

But dusk was falling, and not one of her children or grandchildren had come. It was clear they weren't coming at all. It was almost more than the old woman could bear. As the fire slowly died away to embers, she rocked back and forth, weeping quietly.

She did not know that four of her grown children were only a few yards away, hiding with other slaves in a shed filled with fodder for livestock.

Her daughter, Harriet Tubman, secretly watched the woman through the open cabin door. The firelight made Momma's face bright, and each tear glistened as it ran down her wrinkled cheeks. Harriet was heartbroken that she could not speak to her momma directly.

The smells of the carefully prepared dinner tortured the hungry slaves as they hid in the musty building. Waves of homesickness overwhelmed them, and they longed to go to their parents. They remembered the personal warmth of the weathered cabin and the closeness of the small community of slaves who lived around it.

Harriet was the youngest of ten children born to the now aging couple, Ben and Harriet Ross. She still remembered her early childhood, happy years spent playing on the dirt floor of the cabin. In those days, she was known by her baby name, Minty. She was a young woman now, and her life's work was just beginning. For five years, Harriet had secretly helped slaves travel north to freedom. Tomorrow, she would be leading more out of bondage in Maryland, and this time some were members of her own family.

They had all come to say good-bye, but as they approached their parents' cabin, Harriet realized the emotional scene created by their announcement would be noticed. If anyone found them there, it would jeopardize all their lives, including the lives of their parents.

Harriet sighed. She wished they could celebrate the birth of the Baby Jesus all together with the old folks, but she needed these few days without work to put some distance between her runaways and their masters. She wanted them to be far down the road toward freedom before they were missed.

For now, they hid in the shed, resting up for a long, dangerous journey, mostly on foot, through parts of Maryland, Delaware, New Jersey, and into Pennsylvania.

Two of the men, John and Peter, were not related to Harriet. Once darkness fell, they knocked on the cabin door, intending to ask for food. Old Poppa Ross came to the door and stepped outside to talk with the men, leaving his sad wife to stare into the remains of the fire and dab at her eyes with a well-worn apron.

Outside, the men spoke softly. "We're friends of Harriet's and your boys," they told Poppa. "They didn't come to you 'cause we're heading north. We're in the shed over yonder right now, and your children don't dare come out to be seen. But they want to say good-bye. And we need food real bad."

The old man understood immediately. Calmly, he slipped back into the cabin and spoke to his wife.

Harriet watched from afar. There was no change in her momma's expression. Apparently, the old man hadn't told her their children were nearby. Harriet smiled at that wise decision. Momma was apt to start shouting, "Glory!" Besides, if she didn't know they were there, she could honestly say so later on.

Poppa bundled up some food in a gunnysack and followed the other men away from the cabin.

When they were close to the shed, Poppa said, "Blindfold me."

The younger men looked at each other. Was this old man crazy?

"I say blindfold me and make it tight, young fellas."

One man pulled out his bandana, rolled it into a long strip, and tied it over the old man's eyes. Then they led him into the shed where his children were hiding.

Harriet and her brothers spent time with their father that

Christmas Day. They ate and talked, but the old man never took off his blindfold.

The next day, rested and carrying food for the journey, Harriet and the escaping slaves headed north.

Old Poppa knew that when his children were discovered missing, he would be questioned, and Poppa was a devout Christian who would not lie. Sure enough, a few days later, he and Momma were called to the master's house, which everyone called the Big House, for questioning.

Momma knew nothing. "I looked for them all day," she said sadly. "They never did come."

"Did you see your children before they left, old man?" the law asked Poppa.

"No," he said. "I ain't seen my children in months."

And it was true. He had talked to his children; he had eaten with them, but he had not *seen* them before they escaped to freedom. And he knew he might never see any of them again.

It gave him great satisfaction to know that his beloved little Minty had grown up to become the courageous Harriet Tubman. Her path had been long and hard, but now she acted with the assurance of one watched over by the Lord Himself. Poppa Ross never doubted that she would succeed in escorting her runaways to the safety of Canada. There they would be slaves no more.

But he suspected that Harriet would be back. She had always come back to them before. Even the heavy hand of slavery had not been able to separate her from them for long.

CHAPTER 1

A layer of fog settled over the saltwater marshes of eastern Maryland. Moving slowly through the silver haze was a wagon drawn by one beaten-down old horse. A young white woman held the reins, and tucked in the back sat a six-year-old slave girl called Minty. She shivered in her sack dress in the damp fog. Her soft brown eyes blinked in terror, for Minty had just been sold.

Not an hour before, she'd been dragged crying from her momma and poppa, carried screaming from the only home she'd ever known, a slave cabin on the land of Master Edward Brodas in Dorchester County. Now she was on her way to this stranger's house. The woman needed some kind of help with her work at home, but she was not well off. The only slave she and her husband could afford to buy from the master was a child—Minty.

Where's she gonna take me? Minty thought. *What they gonna do with me?* Horrible scenes paraded through her mind, drawn from whispered nighttime conversations she had overheard and only half-remembered or understood. Were white people really ghosts? Would they beat her? Kill her? One frightful image faded into the next as her heart pounded with terror.

In the early 1800s, at the time Minty was born, black people had much to fear in America. Whether they lived in the Northern or Southern states, most of them were slaves. The few blacks who were free did not have the same rights that

159

most white people took for granted. Even in the North, there were all sorts of restrictions on where they could live, what jobs they could hold, and who they could marry.

The Southern states had a huge and rapidly increasing population of slaves. As the number of black slaves increased, white people became more and more fearful of a black uprising that would kill thousands of white men, women, and children.

Some white masters didn't like slavery but believed they didn't have any choice about having slaves. The entire Southern way of life was dependent on slavery. Life revolved around the huge, wealthy farms called plantations, which grew acres and acres of cotton and tobacco. These plantations needed hundreds of slaves to do all the work. The blacks farmed the land, cared for the livestock, cooked the food, cleaned the clothes, and performed innumerable other tasks for their masters. *Without slaves,* their owners wondered, *how could the plantations survive?*

Slaves owned nothing, not even themselves. Slaves were bought and sold as if they were objects or animals. The life of a slave was full of uncertainty, because if the fields did not produce and the master of the plantation did not prosper, he might feel the need to sell some slaves for extra cash. Kinder masters tried to keep families together, but not all masters were kind. Wives were often sold and separated from their husbands. Children like Minty were routinely sold as well. It was a sad day at the plantation when any slave was sold, but when families were split up, the grief was especially great.

Whether a master was kind or not, the life of a slave was one of poverty, fear, and brutally hard work. Slaves were dependent on the generosity of their masters for food, clothing, shelter, and medical care. No master was particularly generous in those areas.

Slaves usually lived in one-room shacks with dirt floors and no windows. The cabins were cold in the winter and hot in the summer. The only heat came from a fireplace that smoked up the cabin, and this was where all the cooking was done, as well. Most slaves had one outfit to wear—one dress or one pair of pants and a shirt.

The life of a slave was strictly regulated. Slaves could not simply come and go as they pleased. They needed written permission to travel from place to place. They were discouraged from meeting together in large numbers. Even religious meetings in the slave quarters were sometimes frowned upon.

It was illegal to teach a slave to read and write, although the wives and daughters of some plantation owners taught their house slaves to read the Bible. The workday for most slaves stretched from before the sun rose to after it set.

Under such conditions, it was inevitable that some slaves would run away. When they did, they were hunted down like animals, with large packs of dogs. Occasionally, a slave escaped and was never heard from again. Most runaways, however, were quickly recaptured and whipped severely to punish them and to make an example of them so that others would be too frightened to try the same thing. Punishment and the fear of punishment were the main weapons white Southerners used to maintain their power over the blacks who lived in their midst.

Araminta Ross, as Minty was named at her birth around 1820, had already learned more than she ever wanted to know about this life of slavery, even in the few years she had been alive. One thing she never learned was her birthday, because such records were not normally kept for slaves.

Minty never doubted the love of her parents, who had already lost two other young daughters when their master sold them to a chain gang. Her parents were fiercely determined to protect her as much as possible from the suffering of their bondage. They worked hard to include her in the love of their large family. They taught her about their love for God and encouraged her to think of Jesus as her personal friend.

The entire community of slaves on the plantation helped Minty to find joy in the simple details of daily life and to hope for a better life in the world to come. It seemed this world held a grim future for baby Minty because slave life was so hard. Most of all, the other slaves had taught her to express her sorrows and hopes in worship to God and to find comfort and inspiration in God's love for her.

Some plantation owners allowed their slaves to gather for church services. Others found any gathering too threatening. The slaves, they feared, would use the time to plan their escape or, even worse, to plot the murder of their masters. Where they were not allowed to worship openly, slaves often met in secret in what they called brush arbors—areas of dense pine thickets where the boughs would absorb sound. Even the fear of the whip could not keep them from praising Jesus out loud.

As Minty bounced along in the wagon, she looked up at the pearl gray sky and called out to her closest friend. *Oh, Jesus, watch over me,* she prayed.

She knew Momma was praying for her at this very minute. She'd heard her momma pray every time a slave disappeared, whether the slave had been sold or was suspected to have run away.

"Jesus, protect Your children down here," Momma would pray fervently in the privacy of their one-room cabin. "Protect them! Make them strong; make them swift. Make them do right by You. Make them free." Then Momma would rock and moan. It was kind of like singing, but it was softer and seemed full of all the hurt in the world.

Until today, Minty had just watched her momma express those deep longings, while praying so hard it seemed likely to tear her soul from her body. But today Minty was learning to make some of those fervent prayers her own. Though Minty was still a child, she had grown years in her understanding of the world around her in just the last few hours.

She thought of the songs she'd heard sung in the slave quarters, songs the masters had decided were too dangerous and might cause a slave to think of freedom and personal dignity. At first, Minty had not been able to figure that out. How could it be dangerous to sing about wanting to go to glory and be with Jesus?

And what was wrong with singing about the stories in the Bible? Since most slaves could not read, Bible stories were told aloud and sung. Minty loved the songs about Moses leading the Israelites out of Egypt through all kinds of dangers to get to the Promised Land. She'd hear the grown-ups sing from the depths of their souls:

"If I could I surely would
    Stand on the rock where Moses stood.
Pharaoh's army got drown-ded.
    Oh, Mary, don't you weep."

Or perhaps they would shout out Minty's favorite:

"Go down, Moses,
  Way down in Egypt land.
Tell ole Pharaoh
  Let My people go!"

Minty loved the songs. Sometimes they were sung softly in the cabin, and sometimes the field hands sang them loud and strong and in unison to help them get through the long day's toil. She knew what the songs were about: A day would come when Jesus would come again to take them away and make everything right. Then the lion would lie down with the lamb, and the bondage of slavery would no longer have a hold on them.

Even as a little slip of a girl, Minty understood that slavery was evil. Some Christian masters read their Bibles differently on that topic, and white folks all over the world discussed to no end whether or not slavery should continue to exist. But the slaves knew the good Lord had never intended them to be imprisoned in this life of fear and suffering.

Minty was still a little too young to understand that the songs she loved had a second meaning to black folks. They spoke of freedom. Sometimes they told of being freed from slavery by dying and going on to heaven, and sometimes they told about being alive and taking the actual journey north to liberty.

Minty would hear someone sing, "Oh, Canaan, sweet Canaan, I am bound for the land of Canaan," and the sweet sounds seemed full of mystery to her. She had only recently been able to tell the words Canaan and Canada apart; they felt so alike rolling off her Southern tongue. Just last week, Momma had explained that Canaan was the Promised Land in the Bible, but Canada was a snowy land way up north where blacks could not be held as slaves.

"Either one says freedom," Poppa had muttered as he poked at the fire with a stick.

Momma had given him a stern look out of the corner of her eye. "You hush," she scolded gently. Though the cabin felt warm, cozy, and safe, they could never be sure who might be listening outside. And it wouldn't be good to let the master know there was freedom talk going on in the quarters.

Go down, Moses, Minty sang to herself as the wagon slowed. She wrapped her thin brown arms around her body. *Oh, Lord, be with me,* she prayed over and over.

The wagon turned off onto a narrower dirt road she had never seen before, and Minty felt numb with both cold and fear. A small log house with a fence around it appeared. It didn't look anything like the Big House. It sat in a clearing in the woods, and Minty could smell the river nearby, but she had no idea where she was. She'd never left the Brodases' plantation before and had no idea what to expect.

CHAPTER 2

At her new home, Minty was expected to help the young married mistress, Mrs. Cook, with her work as a weaver. She worked at home on a spinning wheel and loom, while Mr. Cook trapped fish and hunted animals for a living. The Cooks owned very little land and were not at all wealthy, but their log house was still the biggest one Minty had ever been in. She'd never set foot in the Big House on the Brodases' plantation when she had lived with her parents.

Though the Cooks' house had more than one room, Minty was expected to sleep on the floor next to the kitchen fireplace, as if she were a dog. They fed her about as much as they'd feed a dog, too. The Cooks wanted a willing and productive worker, but they were unwilling to spend even one cent more than it took to just barely keep their new slave alive.

Minty's job was to wind yarn while Mrs. Cook worked the wheel and loom. Yarn fuzz constantly got into Minty's nose and mouth, making her sneeze or cough. As hard as she tried, she couldn't perform her task properly, and she hated every minute of it. She was afraid of the Cooks because of their cruelty. Constant hunger pains dominated her waking hours, and she slept fitfully on the cold, hard floor. Most of all, she was homesick. Mrs. Cook scolded Minty constantly but never lifted a finger to improve her living conditions. Naturally, Minty's work continued to be clumsy and slow.

Finally, Mrs. Cook handed Minty over to Mr. Cook. "See if she's any help to you outside. She's no use to me."

Mr. Cook showed Minty how to tend the muskrat traps in the river while he hunted elsewhere. The animals were highly valued for their fur. Minty moved back and forth, watching the line of baskets in the cold water. When she found a trapped muskrat, it took all her young strength to haul it out of the river. Some days it was so cold, she could hardly feel her bare feet.

In spite of the cold, Minty was relieved to be out of the house and off by herself. She'd learned to appreciate God's natural world from Poppa.

Although Poppa had never been allowed to learn to read, he was the smartest man Minty knew. He could predict the weather for the next day or the next season simply by watching the sky or observing animals in the woods. He knew which herbs and plants were poisonous and which were useful for healing. He understood how the phases of the moon could be used as a guide for successful farming or fishing. He was familiar with the shapes of all the constellations in the night sky, and he showed his daughter how they moved with the seasons.

In particular, he pointed out the North Star. It held a special meaning for Poppa and all other slaves, though it was seldom spoken of openly. As the long days and hungry nights dragged on, Minty began to understand his passion for that one stationary point of light: The North Star led to freedom.

In the half-light just before dawn, Minty would often look for the North Star and think of Momma and Poppa. She knew they were trapped just like those river muskrats. As Minty prayed for a change in all their lives, a dream of freedom grew in the secret places of her soul.

The first step down the road toward her dream almost killed her. Minty came down with the measles. At the time when she lived, many illnesses could kill a child, but measles was one of the deadliest.

In spite of Minty's fever and weakness, the Cooks insisted that she continue wading barefoot in the cold river to haul in the heavy baskets with their trapped muskrats.

The fever increased, and Minty developed severe bronchitis. She grew weaker, and every breath was painful. One day she simply collapsed. The Cooks wrapped her in a blanket and left her alone.

Among the slaves who worked on the great plantations and even among those who worked for less wealthy owners, an amazing network of personal communication existed. All the white masters understood that the slaves knew more about what was going on in the Big House, and knew it sooner, than the white folks who lived there did. And news about the slaves themselves always traveled rapidly from one place to another. Word about Minty's serious illness was quickly relayed to the Brodas plantation.

Momma Ross went to Master Brodas and begged to have her child back. "That child's gonna die if I don't nurse her back to health myself," Momma insisted.

Master Brodas was moved by her plea and sent for Mr. Cook and Minty. "Let her people make her well," he told Mr. Cook. "I don't know how they do it, but they usually succeed. Then I'll send her back to you."

Mr. Cook was relieved. If Minty died, he would lose his investment, and he didn't want that. He agreed wholeheartedly to the plan and went home, leaving Minty behind.

Minty was carried back to her momma's cabin. With the help of potions homemade from the herbs Poppa gathered in the woods, she slowly regained her health. Momma made Minty eat until she couldn't hold anymore. It was clear the Cooks weren't feeding her much. Finally, she was healthy enough to return to the Cooks' house.

However, the effects of severe bronchitis at such a young age forever altered Minty's voice. It became deep and husky, not like a child's at all. For the rest of her life, people could identify her by the distinct sound of her voice shouting out the cadences of a work song, praising Jesus in worship, or whispering words of freedom in the night.

Back at the Cooks', things were as bad as before—even worse since Minty was now seen as too weak to work outdoors. Once again she took up weaving work, though she still had no heart for it and was just as clumsy as before. Finally, the Cooks gave up on her and took her back to Brodas. They claimed she was stupid and lazy.

"We aren't about to keep feeding someone who won't work," Mrs. Cook insisted, her voice full of self-righteous scorn.

Minty was happy to be back living with her parents in their small cabin in the slave quarters on the Brodas plantation. Though she was now only seven and considered sickly, she was still expected to work. All slaves worked from the time they were old enough to leave their mothers. Even the littlest ones carried water to the field hands.

Momma and Poppa Ross were worried that Minty had become too much of a problem for the master and that he might sell her off. He'd done it before with two of their small daughters. The Rosses didn't think they could bear that again, especially with their youngest and smartest child, Minty.

But times were ripe for another big slave sale on the plantation. To keep up his standard of living, Mr. Brodas needed cash. When the crops weren't good—and they hadn't been lately—he sold timber from his forest. And slaves.

More and more plantations were supporting themselves by breeding, raising, and selling slaves, as if the slaves were nothing more than horses. And the chain gangs kept stopping by, looking for new slaves to replace the ones that had died through neglect and overwork. The community of people living in the slave quarters was constantly threatened with the loss of relatives and friends.

Fortunately, little Minty wasn't snapped up by a chain gang, but Master Brodas did sell her once more. This time she went to a relatively prosperous family living in another Big House.

Her new mistress was called Miss Susan, and Minty, still a little girl, was to take care of Miss Susan's only child. Minty was so small for her age that she couldn't hold the baby properly while sitting or standing, so she would sit on the floor and hold the child in her lap. Minty became a living cradle for the baby. And the child stayed in Minty's lap all day unless Miss Susan was feeding him.

At night, when the baby slept in a real cradle, Minty slept on the floor nearby. Or rather, didn't sleep. She was expected to rock the cradle anytime the baby cried and help him get back to sleep. And this was an especially fussy baby. Minty soon learned how to drift in and out of sleep while rocking the cradle constantly.

Minty was also expected to help Miss Susan keep the

house clean and care for the furniture. This quickly became a nightmare.

Minty had never lived anywhere but in log cabins. She had never even seen anything like the polished furniture, carved wood, and carpets that filled the many rooms in this Big House. Minty had grown up playing on a dirt floor in her parents' cabin. Even at the Cooks', she had slept next to ashes in the fireplace. When Miss Susan told her to dust, Minty had no idea what that meant.

Her life had always included a little dirt, dust, and ash. Poppa used to say, "We all eat a bushel of dirt 'fore we die." The life-giving earth and the warming fire were friends to be accepted, not enemies to be fought. Why would anyone try to remove all traces of them?

Minty had no idea how to care for this woman's house. She didn't even know what questions to ask. From the very beginning, she was terrified of making mistakes, just as she had been at the Cooks'.

Miss Susan made a difficult situation impossible because she was neither patient nor kind. Rather than trying to help Minty by explaining how things were done, she reacted to Minty's lack of knowledge by calling her stupid. When harsh words brought no changes, she quickly brought out a whip and began whipping Minty. Fortunately, Miss Susan's sister intervened, severely scolding her sister for whipping a child. Then the sister carefully taught Minty how to clean a house.

Even after her sister's tongue-lashing, Miss Susan still enjoyed using that whip. If the baby cried, she whipped Minty. If the house wasn't kept spotless, she whipped Minty.

One day, Miss Susan caught Minty "stealing" a lump of sugar from the sugar bowl. Out came the whip, but this time

Minty ran. She had already taken as much abuse as she could stand. She ran crying through the house, pushing startled servants and family members aside. Out the front door she rushed and sprinted for the nearby woods, trying to find a place to hide from her tormentor. Miss Susan and her husband chased her for a little ways, but finally gave up.

Minty stayed in hiding until hunger and thirst began to eat away at her. For several days, she hid in a pigpen, fighting with the pigs for food and water. Even though she loved the outdoors, she had no idea how to survive on her own. She had never learned enough about the lay of the land to find her way back to the Brodas plantation and seek shelter with her momma and poppa.

Eventually, she came out of hiding and dragged herself back to her mistress. Minty was hungry, filthy, and frightened that Miss Susan might kill her. Miss Susan almost did.

This whipping was the most severe Minty had ever received. When Miss Susan had worn herself out from screaming and beating the child with the short rawhide whip, she left Minty lying on the ground near the back of the house, bleeding from deep tears on her back, and nearly unconscious from pain. Then Miss Susan went to fetch her husband. Together, they decided to take Minty back to Master Brodas and ask for their money back. They had the same complaints as the Cooks —that Minty was stupid and lazy.

Master Brodas turned Minty over to her momma again, this time to heal the bleeding whip marks that crisscrossed numerous older scars.

Momma had seldom been as angry with the white folks as she was now. Even so, she only spoke of it within the relative safety of the cabin walls. Sometimes she talked to Poppa about it, but usually she just cried out to the Lord. "Whipping a child like this. Don't feed her, don't clean her up, and then they whip her like a dog."

While she talked, Momma sponged cool, herbal teas onto Minty's back and neck. "What's gonna come of my baby, dear Jesus?" she asked in an anguished voice. "Lord, make her strong. Protect this child. Work Your mysterious ways in her life." Then she softly sang and cried.

Minty slept soundly on her stomach for days, letting her wounds heal and making up for all that sleep she'd lost rocking the white baby's cradle and fighting with hungry pigs. Momma's comforting voice floated through Minty's dreams, and she knew, even asleep, that she was safe. When she was awake, Momma fed her corn bread and rich goat's milk to fatten her up a little and give her strength.

While Minty was getting her health back, Master Brodas let Momma know that he wasn't going to sell Minty again. This time, he wanted to hire her out. This would allow her to continue living at the plantation while she worked for someone nearby. Momma was glad Minty would be staying with them, but she was worried about how she would do in her new job. She had hoped Minty could learn a useful indoor trade so that she could live an easier life as a household slave. Master Brodas wanted to hire her out as a field hand, even though she was not yet ten years old.

"What You got in mind, Lord?" Momma prayed. "You better help her hold up in that hot sun, Lord. Teach her how to earn her keep. Please don't let her go away on the chain gang."

Then she rocked and moaned as her Minty slept next to her, safe and sound—for that day, at least.

CHAPTER 3

The sun beat down mercilessly as Minty tried to reason with a mule. Years had passed, and she was now a valued field hand. Her instinctive knowledge of animals and her love for all things in the outdoors were unique skills that gave her a special status, even as a slave.

Her skinny frame had filled out, giving her the lean muscular body of a strong young woman. Her arms, legs, and shoulders had hardened like a man's. Though she never grew over five feet tall, her back was straight and strong. Her bare feet and her hardworking hands were protected by layers of tough calluses.

Minty had long since stopped wearing a child's sack garment. Now she wore a woman's dress, which she managed to twist into something like trousers when necessary in the field. She also wore a colorful bandana tied around her head, like the other grown women.

Minty was expected to lift, pick, push, and plow like a man. And she rose to the occasion because she loved to be outdoors. Even while she was working, there was time to study the landscape, the birds, and the river. Her deep, husky voice often joined those of her fellow workers in songs that would rise up out of the fields and soar above the trees, straight on up to Jesus.

Every day of breathing fresh air instead of wool lint or soiled diapers made Minty grateful to God. The Lord did indeed work in mysterious ways. What Momma had thought was all wrong on the master's part had actually been right for Minty. The Lord's hand had brought her to this work, she knew.

She began to sing a song written by a man who spent years kidnaping and selling slaves until the day when Jesus showed him what a terrible thing he was doing. People said the man never sold another slave. Sometimes, Minty wondered what kinds of changes God had in store for her life.

"Amazing grace, how sweet the sound
    That saved a wretch like me. . ."

The rest of the field hands joined her:

"I once was lost but now am found,
    Was blind but now I see."

After several verses, the song died away. Sometimes, singing was the only thing that made their hard work bearable. But today, as Minty tried reasoning with the mule, her song was one of simple praise to God.

A new song started up, and a field hand walked up behind Minty. "You hear about Joe Dubois?" he said softly, counting on the sound of the music to hide his words from the ever-watchful white overseers.

Minty shook her head. She knew Joe, a dark-skinned, gentle giant of a man.

"He heard he was going to the chain gang for big money, and he ran." The field hand pulled at a leather strap on the mule's harness, pretending to adjust it. "He got on that Underground Railroad, Sister. He ain't never gonna work these fields again, praise the Lord." Then he quietly walked away.

Minty kept her hands moving along the mule's harness, but her mind was no longer on the adjustments she needed to make. What was the field hand talking about? She'd seen plenty of trains. Trains were used by white folks, and a few blacks as well, to travel long distances. At night, she could hear their sad whistles from miles away.

But a train under the ground?

It took some time and a lot of whispered questions at night in various slave cabins, but eventually Minty understood the Underground Railroad.

To begin with, it was not a railroad, nor did it run through some big tunnel under the ground. There were white folks who didn't believe in slavery, people who felt the same way about it as the man who wrote the hymn "Amazing Grace." Mostly they lived up North, but some could be found in the South.

These people believed that the living Christ had called them to free all the slaves. Many were Quakers, who wore odd clothing and talked like characters out of some Bible story, using words like "thee" and "thou" when speaking to their friends. Others were Methodists, who were always trying to figure out how God wanted them to act in the smallest details of their daily lives.

All of them believed without a doubt that the Lord had made all humans equal. They also believed that the Constitution of the United States had been written to protect that equality. They were willing to risk their lives to fight the evil of slavery by helping slaves escape to freedom in the North.

Minty had never heard of such white people. She certainly had never known any like that. Miss Susan's sister had shown her a little compassion, and that was surprising in itself. But could it be true that some white folks actually wanted to free all the slaves?

As she carefully questioned other slaves in the fields, she discovered there were many routes that led to the North and freedom. Even slaves in the Deep South could find routes that took them to boats and across the Caribbean Sea.

In Maryland and most other parts of the South, escaping slaves traveled mainly on foot. There were special code words everyone used to describe the system. A "station" was a house that would provide food, shelter, and money. Runaway slaves were called "passengers," and those who guided them along the routes were called "conductors." Once the runaways reached the Northern states, many committed people, both free blacks and whites, would help them start a new life of freedom in this strange new land.

This all sounded like a magical train bound for heaven to Minty, but everyone insisted the Underground Railroad truly existed. You simply had to know the right white person and have the courage to leave your master.

Know white people? Minty thought when she heard this. *And trust white people?* She shook her head. How could she trust people who treated her like an animal, who believed they had the right to own her? That was just plain foolish.

One day, a short time later, Minty was squatting down picking strawberries in the south fields. The sun wasn't so brutally hot, and the berries were coming off the vine as easy as could be. As she dragged her berry basket down the row, Minty thought back over everything she'd heard about the Underground Railroad, with its stations and conductors.

"Trust Me."

Minty looked up. *Who said that?* She straightened her back and looked around. It had been a mature voice, a deep male voice. But there were only women picking nearby, and the overseer was on the far side of the field.

Sometimes, so the old folks said, the hot sun could make people hear or see strange things in the fields. That was why they encouraged new field hands to wear a straw hat in the midday sun. Minty thought about that. She was no newcomer, and there wasn't enough sun to get excited over. She frowned and bent over the next plant.

"Trust Me."

Now she stood up, then quickly squatted back down before the overseer noticed. She began to tremble. "Oh, Lord," she whispered. "You talking to me?"

There was silence. She kept picking strawberries automatically, but her mind grappled wildly with the words she knew she'd heard. The hair on her neck stood up in the same way it did when the hymns in the slave quarters on Sunday were particularly powerful. Could this be the Lord's doing?

"I have always trusted You, Lord," she prayed softly, moving to the next plant.

"Trust Me."

Three times. Even though she could not read, Minty knew enough about the Bible to realize that a command spoken three times was meant to be taken seriously. This was surely a message from God for her to think on and figure out.

She nodded and silently finished her work. If God was going to act on her behalf, if He was asking her to trust His ability to intervene directly in her life, then perhaps her mistrust of white people would make no difference.

"I hear You, Lord," she prayed quietly. "I will trust You to show me the way out of here and the proper time to leave."

By the time she was twelve years old, Minty was as strong as any man on the plantation. She was also short and slim and female, so that neither Master Brodas nor his overseers felt the least bit threatened by her.

Because of her hard work, outward obedience, and lack of chatter, Master Brodas considered Minty a good slave. Many times when her husky, full-voiced singing set the pace for work in the fields, he congratulated himself on his decision to keep her working for his plantation.

But Master Brodas had no idea of the revolution that had taken place in Minty's mind. She was convinced that slavery was wrong, and she was determined to find a way to freedom for herself and all of her people. She was only waiting on the Lord to show her the right time to act.

That fall, during the part of the harvest when the corn was shucked, Minty noticed a slave acting oddly. She glanced around, still stripping the outer leaves off the husks, to see if anyone else noticed. He was shucking very slowly and seemed nervous, even jumpy. That was no way to act around an overseer. Fortunately, the overseer had his back turned to the slave.

Suddenly, the slave broke away from the crowd of workers and ran. He was halfway across the field before the overseer noticed and took off after him, whip in hand.

Usually, overseers did their work mounted. The horse allowed them to intimidate the workers and also to move quickly. But this overseer had been inspecting the harvest on foot, and he was so angry that he hadn't taken the time to go after his horse on the other side of the field. Even so, he was rapidly gaining ground on the fleeing slave.

Minty was terribly frightened for the runaway. Without thinking, she took off after the overseer. She found both men in a dim storage building just beyond the cornfield. The overseer wanted to whip the slave immediately, and when he saw Minty, he ordered her to tie the man to one of the large wooden posts that held up the building's roof. Minty simply stood there and looked at the two men.

Suddenly, the slave darted past her and ran toward the open door. The overseer moved to follow, but Minty blocked his way. The overseer was surprised and frustrated. He wanted to stop the fleeing slave, so he grabbed a two-pound brick and threw it after the man.

The throw was much too short, and the brick hit Minty square in the forehead, knocking her out. She collapsed to the dusty floor with a sickening thud, and a rapidly growing pool of blood appeared around her head.

The slave got away, but Minty's life would never be the same.

CHAPTER 4

Once again, Minty lay on a pallet in her momma's cabin. This time she was unconscious most of the time. It was obvious to everyone that she was near death. The brick had cracked her skull, and there was an ugly, frightening hole in her forehead. She slept and slept.

Even during those parts of the day when she appeared to be awake, she had actually dozed off. For months, Momma Ross worked on her daughter's wound, dressing it with herbs while she worried and prayed over her semiconscious child.

Word of Minty's brave and selfless act that helped a slave escape spread quickly. Because of their admiration for her, the slave community changed her name. They would no longer use her baby name. From now on, she would be called by her mother's name, Harriet. This was a tremendous honor. It was a way people in the quarters could show their respect for one of their own without actually speaking about her act of outright rebellion.

Now there were two questions on everyone's lips. Would young Harriet survive, and what would the master do with her if she did? It didn't look like she'd ever pull out of the stupor she was in, much less return to being the hearty young woman she'd been before her injury.

Momma Ross prayed hard. "Lord, I know You can pull my baby through. And I know You make good from evil. Let Harriet live, and use her life for Your purposes."

November passed, then Christmas. Harriet was still unable

to speak or walk. Winter came and went. Finally, as spring approached and the natural world woke up from its long sleep, so did Harriet. The wound was now a nasty scar. She was actually able to remain conscious for the entire day, though she stayed quiet for several more weeks. Miraculously, Harriet had been given a new life to go with her new name. Her parents thanked the Lord.

When Master Brodas heard Harriet was recovering, he tried to sell her, but prospective buyers just laughed. All they could see was a slave who was physically weak, obviously rebellious, and because of the scar on her forehead, frightening to look at. Although Harriet was on the mend, she still had horrible headaches. The scar itself was painful, and she was prone to fainting spells. She never knew when she would fall into a deep sleep. She had no control over it at all. She could be standing on the dirt path in front of her parents' cabin or be in the middle of a conversation with a friend, and she would simply collapse on the ground, sound asleep. When this happened, no one could wake her up.

During these periods of deep unconsciousness, she would sometimes have detailed visions full of vivid images. As Harriet floated in and out of touch with life in the slave quarters, these visions often seemed more real than her actual surroundings.

With her body slowly healing, she had a lot of time to think about what had happened to her. She was sure that she had been spared—and even changed—for a reason.

At first, she believed God wanted her to pray for Master Brodas. She spent days in prayer, asking God to work on her white master and convert him. She maintained this pattern of nearly continuous prayer for weeks as she lay quietly on her pallet.

Having spent so many hours praying for her master's welfare, it came as a great shock to her when she learned that he was making arrangements to sell her, along with two of her brothers, to a chain gang. Harriet was truly frightened. She was still too weak to survive the terrible conditions the slaves working on chain gangs had to endure. She was even too sick to run away.

Her fear quickly became a dark anger that turned all her thoughts ugly and vengeful. She began praying that God would kill Master Brodas. When her headaches tormented her, these prayers became a steady chanting inside her throbbing head: *Kill him, Lord. Kill him.* She was totally obsessed with the idea of punishing this white man who had done so many evil things to her and her family.

A few days later, Edward Brodas suddenly became ill, and a few days after that, he died.

As soon as Harriet learned of her master's death, she was horrified and guilt-stricken. Though she desperately wanted to believe otherwise, she was sure that her prayers had killed Master Brodas.

A severe headache seized her, and she collapsed onto her pallet in the cabin, curling into a shaking ball of pain. With what little strength she had left, she begged God for forgiveness and asked for opportunities to do good in the world around her.

One day she would understand that Master Brodas had not died because of her prayers, but for now she was filled with remorse. Though Harriet firmly believed in the power of prayer for the rest of her long life, she could never again bring herself to pray that anything evil should happen to another human being.

The death of Edward Brodas was followed by a time of confusion and mourning. There was no way to anticipate what his heir would do with the plantation and its slaves. Sometimes a change of ownership meant that all the slaves were sold, often breaking up families.

As the slaves on the Brodas plantation sang their long, slow songs of mourning far into the night, they were expressing their own worries for the future, as well as paying their respects to their master's memory.

Fortunately, the heir was a doctor and minister who decided to leave the plantation and its workforce largely undisturbed. In the future, if slaves had to be sold, they would only go to owners living in the state of Maryland. Everyone in the quarters breathed a little easier.

In time, Harriet recovered enough of her strength to perform household tasks and was hired out to a man named Stewart. After a short while, she insisted that she was feeling much better and appealed to Stewart for more outside work. Stewart agreed to let her be a field hand again and soon discovered that Harriet could do just as much work as any man. However, because she was a woman, Stewart didn't have to pay as much for her labor.

The hard work in the fields made Harriet even stronger than she had been before her injury. She grew so strong that Master Stewart would invite his friends over to watch her lift and throw heavy items. Later he developed a surprise ending for his demonstrations. Harriet would put on a special harness and tow a barge down the river while walking along the bank.

His friends loved the show, but Harriet felt like an animal doing tricks.

Master Stewart was so pleased with Harriet that he allowed her free time to hire herself out. The money she made was hers to keep. Harriet also had numerous opportunities to help her poppa cut timber in the woods. She gained a whole new appreciation for this quietly wise man.

He picked right up where he had left off years ago and continued teaching his daughter everything he knew about nature. Harriet sensed a new urgency in his lessons. Poppa Ross knew his daughter was too special not to be free, and he wanted to give her the knowledge she would need to escape someday. Though they never spoke of this openly, Harriet came to understand his real goal.

Poppa showed Harriet which herbs were valuable as medicines and explained how to use them in healing. He pointed out the roots and berries that were edible and warned her about those that were dangerous.

He taught her as much as he knew about the geography of Maryland—information about rivers, marshes, and forests, as well as the locations of major roads and towns. She soon realized that he had learned a great deal on his many trips with Master Brodas away from the plantation.

Poppa showed Harriet how to find her way through the darkest forest at night using the stars as a compass. And he reminded her that the North Star still pointed the way to freedom.

Most important, Poppa Ross taught Harriet how to move quietly in the woods. "A forest is a noisy thing when you listen to it," Poppa explained. The perfect beauty of God's world had been stained by human rebellion in the Garden of Eden. Poppa believed that one result of that tragedy was the unnecessary noise that constantly disturbed the peace of the natural world.

Harriet learned to listen for twigs breaking, birds chirping, owls hooting, deer scampering, rabbits scurrying, and branches crashing to the forest floor. Poppa taught her not only how to listen to sounds and interpret them, but also how to mimic hoot owls and other birds.

Finally, he helped her to listen for the noises she made in the woods, and then he showed her how to eliminate them. Soon she could glide through the trees like a shadow. She even managed to creep up on her old father and startle him a few times. Each time he was pleased with her, very pleased, and a hopeful light began to grow in his eyes.

Life went on without any serious problems for several years in the Ross family. Harriet continued to work hard and hire herself out for some money of her own.

But as she moved into her twenties, Harriet found that something in her life was missing. She found herself listening to the mourning doves and their plaintive songs.

"Mourning dove crying for rain," Momma had always told her. But the field hands said, "Mourning dove crying for its mate."

A mate. A husband. That's what was missing. Harriet was aware of soft new feelings—a desire to marry a good man, maybe have children. For the first time, she shyly observed the men around her in a different light. She wondered who might make a suitable husband.

When a man called John Tubman noticed Harriet, she knew her quest for love was finished. Serious young Harriet found a balance to her somber personality in this handsome, laughing man. Maybe the fact that John was a free man made him that much more appealing. At any rate, Harriet fell in love.

Slaves didn't have weddings or legal marriages in the manner of white folks. But slaves did have a marriage ceremony called "jumping the broom." Slaves who wished to marry asked permission of the master, and if he agreed to the union, the betrothed and their families would gather around a broom lying on the floor. Then the couple would jump together over the broom. This symbolized their commitment to each other. Sometimes, if the master was a more devout Christian man, he would make certain there was a religious ceremony for the new couple.

In 1844, John Tubman and Harriet Ross were married, making a commitment to spend the rest of their lives together. Harriet left her parents' cabin and moved in with her new husband.

In 1846, a family of slaves by the name of Crosswhite traveled secretly from Kentucky to a way station on the Underground Railroad in the small Northern town of Marshall, Michigan. That part of Michigan was being settled mostly by New Yorkers who left everything behind them and had traveled down the Erie Canal looking for good farmland.

These New Yorkers brought with them a deep hatred of slavery. Because of this, Michigan became a final destination for many slaves from Kentucky and other nearby slave states. The Crosswhite family, like many fugitive families, was grateful for the hospitality of the citizens of Marshall and decided to settle there.

One day, slavers from Kentucky appeared and demanded to take the Crosswhite family back to the plantation from which they had escaped. But the leaders of Marshall had the constables arrest the slavers on the charge of kidnaping and throw them in jail.

By the time the Kentuckians were released, the Crosswhite family had been spirited across Michigan and were on their way to Canada.

This was one of countless stories of heroism that encouraged slaves in their quest for freedom. It was also one of many incidents that would eventually cause Congress to draft and pass the Fugitive Slave Law in 1850, which would say that runaway slaves could be returned to the South, and make it a crime to help runaways even in the free soil of the North.

Harriet always listened for any encouraging tidbits of news regarding runaway slaves. John Tubman was free because his parents had been freed after their master's death. But she, his wife, was a slave. Her entire family were slaves. She could be sold whether or not her husband was free, and if that happened, she might never see John or any of her family members again.

One night, she told John about the Crosswhites in Michigan. Her eyes were alight with excitement, though she kept her voice low. She began to speak to him about running away together.

John Tubman, usually good-natured, became very agitated. He had his freedom already, and he did not think it necessary for Harriet to be free. Most of all, he did not want her to do anything that would jeopardize their fairly comfortable way of life.

This shocked Harriet. "But John," she said, "you're a free man. Don't you want that for me? Don't you want children someday and have them be free?"

"We're all right just the way we are," John declared angrily. "I make my own money, and you're able to hire out for money, too. We got our own place. We aren't so bad off."

But things weren't all that good, either. Times were hard on the plantation. Cotton prices were going down, and everyone knew what that meant—more slaves would be sold to the chain gang. Harriet was terrified it would happen to her.

She appealed to her husband again. "Please, John," she whispered, "I know we can do this. Slaves go north all the time. There's a way. Then nobody would ever be able to separate us!" John Tubman simply shook his head.

Harriet started having a series of dreams at night. In them, she could see and hear the terrors of slaves being rousted out of their cabins at night and sold. She could see and hear the chain gang trudging, their irons clanking, the slaves weeping. Then she dreamed she was swimming across a river. Just as she was about to go down in the deep water and drown, women dressed in white reached out, grabbed her flailing arms, and pulled her across.

She decided the first dream was a warning from God that she was going to be sold, and the second dream was a comfort from God that she should head north, and His angels would watch over her. She decided to approach John again about running away by telling him about the dreams.

First he laughed at her. Then he became angry again. "Put this running away out of your head, Harriet."

"But John, they gonna sell me someday. You and me will never see each other again."

John Tubman did not respond to that. He simply bent down and put his face close to hers. It almost seemed like he was growling. "If you run, I'll tell the master."

Harriet stepped back. "You would tell on your own wife?"

"I'd tell him as fast as I could." John pounded his fist in his hand. Then he folded his arms and glared down at her.

"You know what they do to runaways," Harriet whispered. "You would let them do that to me?"

"Try running and see," he said. She looked deep into his eyes and saw no love there. For the first time, Harriet was afraid of John.

Harriet was terribly hurt to discover that her own husband would betray her to the master. Yet John Tubman was the only man Harriet had ever loved, and even the hurt he caused her could not kill her love for him.

But she knew the Lord wanted to help her be free, always had known it. She was also certain that the time would come when John would see it her way. Then she would come back for him. But that time was not now. Harriet became even more determined to leave. She not only watched for the right time to escape, but she also watched John closely so that he would not know of her plans. She did not doubt for a minute that he would turn on her.

By 1849, three years after the Crosswhite affair in Michigan, enough time had elapsed without Harriet leaving that John Tubman no longer seemed suspicious. Harriet noted it and was relieved. But it wasn't yet time to leave.

One day, a white woman approached Harriet while she was working in the fields near the road. Harriet had never looked at white people's faces much. In the South, blacks did not look whites in the eyes, and Harriet found their faces frightening anyway. They seemed to have no insides, no warmth.

But she found herself looking directly at the white woman. She was old and had the kindest face Harriet had seen except for her own mother's. This old woman had straight, thin white hair parted neatly in the center, eyes as gray as a spring rain cloud, and soft-looking skin with blue veins showing at her temples. She wore a simple dress and bonnet, the attire of a farmer's wife. She was very clean and crisp.

The old woman had reined in her horse and turned in her wagon to face Harriet. She smiled, looking right into Harriet's eyes, and began chatting about the day, the weather, and the crops. The woman was friendly and talkative, and for the first time in her life, Harriet found herself talking normally and naturally to someone who was not black. This woman seemed be a decent person.

Suddenly, Harriet remembered God telling her in the strawberry field to trust Him. It had been years. What was going to happen? Did it have something to do with this white woman? For the time being, Harriet decided simply to get to know the woman better. They chatted a couple times each week at the side of the road.

Suddenly, things started to change on the plantation. Slaves were being sold off. Before anyone knew what was happening, two of Harriet's sisters were gone on the chain gang. Her parents were mortified. Panic filled the slave quarters.

Harriet found herself sharing the news with her new white friend. The woman never hesitated. She quietly said, "If you ever need anything, Harriet—anything at all—you know where I live. You hear me?"

Harriet nodded, and the old woman rode off on her wagon. *Maybe,* Harriet thought, *the women dressed in white in the dreams represented white women instead of angels.*

The time had come, Harriet decided, to run for it. But she was afraid to go alone. She didn't dare tell John, but she did ask three of her brothers to go with her. They agreed, and plans were made.

On the night of their escape, Harriet waited until John was asleep. Then she met her brothers near the fields. Off they went.

But after only a mile, her brothers' fears got the better of them. They decided to go back. Furthermore, they forced their baby sister to return with them.

Harriet was angry with her brothers, and she realized that

if she was going to escape, she'd have to do it alone. She'd just have to wait for the right time. She slipped back into her cabin. Fortunately, John was sound asleep and hadn't noticed she'd left.

The right time came two days later when a field hand told Harriet that he'd just learned the chain gang was taking Harriet and her three brothers that very night. Now she knew she'd have to leave as soon as it was dark.

There was plenty about the upcoming journey to frighten Harriet. The lack of food and shelter, the fact that she'd never traveled anywhere alone before, the need to travel only at night and stay hidden during the day, the threat of being hunted down by bloodhounds and returned to be whipped—all these were good reasons to be afraid.

But it was also her own body that Harriet had to consider. She was afraid it would betray her. Her scar made her easily recognizable. She had an unusually lean yet muscular build for a woman, and nobody who ever heard her deep voice could forget it. Her headaches and blackouts could come at any time. She might be crossing a road in full view of anyone and fall into a deep sleep. Or she could be crossing a river and drown because of a blackout.

In the middle of her panic, Harriet felt the assurance of the Lord settle over her. She believed this journey was blessed. She would trust in the Lord. He would see her through.

That night Harriet rose in the dark and tied some food up in a kerchief. Then she left the cabin and John Tubman. It hurt to leave the only man she'd ever loved, even if he didn't love her as much as she'd hoped he did. But she also felt she had no choice. She simply could not be sold to a chain gang, never to see any of her loved ones again.

She left the plantation by way of the back of the Big House where Harriet's sister was a cook. Because of the hot weather and the heat of cooking, the kitchen on a plantation was in a separate building a few steps from the Big House. Staying well outside the kitchen where her sister was working, Harriet composed a song on the spot and sang it so the sister would know where she'd be:

> "Good-bye, I'm going to leave you,
>   Good-bye, I'll meet you in the kingdom. . . ."

And so Harriet set out for freedom. Her first stop was the old white woman's house. The woman didn't seem the least bit surprised to see Harriet. She sat Harriet down and explained the Underground Railroad more fully to her, then she wrote two names on a piece of paper.

"These are the next places for you to stop," she said. "You'll be safe there. I'll tell you how to get to the first one, and you show them this paper. They'll tell you how to get to the next stop. There will be many stops like these where people will feed you and shelter you and direct you. Soon enough, you'll be in Philadelphia."

Harriet felt a bit rattled, but when the kind old woman offered to pray over her, she calmed down. She remembered the dreams and the words of the Lord: *"Trust Me."*

Finally, she said good-bye to the first white person she would call friend, and Harriet Tubman headed for the woods, following the North Star.

CHAPTER 6

Harriet's destination was Philadelphia, Pennsylvania, where there was a network of freed slaves and other concerned people to help her start a new life. Fortunately, Maryland, where Harriet lived, was fairly close to Pennsylvania—about ninety miles. But she would still have to travel many miles on foot during several days and nights of uncertainty and fear.

Harriet left the old woman's house in the dark of night, and she used all her knowledge of the woods to get her through that dark forest. She kept moving all night, quickly, quickly. Every step was one more step away from the bloodhounds and the whip. With every step she prayed, "I trust You, Lord. . .I trust You, Lord." It became a hopeful rhythm for her as she moved through the trees and the underbrush.

And somehow by the end of that first night, Harriet lost her fear. She kept her wits about her, but her fear was gone, never to return in full measure. Years later, "fearless" was one of the words that everyone who knew Harriet would use to describe her.

The next morning she found the farmhouse the old woman had described. She handed her piece of paper to the woman who answered the kitchen door, and the woman smiled. "Come and eat," she said.

Harriet hadn't realized how hungry she was. She ate bacon and home-baked biscuits with blueberry preserves. The food was delicious, and it was a new experience for Harriet, a slave all her life, to be fed by a white woman. After breakfast, the

woman handed her a broom and suggested she sweep the
yard. Folks in the South often had dirt yards that they would
sweep into pretty patterns. Harriet had swept yards often in
her childhood, and she did so now, happily. She realized that
the law would never suspect a slave who was working out in
the open of being a runaway.

She left the farm that night on the floor of the farmer's
produce wagon, covered with a blanket and a load of fresh
vegetables. She thought wistfully about her family and what
would be happening back home. She dozed and dreamed and
marveled that the Lord had taken away her fear.

The wagon stopped at a river in the dark hours of early
morning. The farmer gave Harriet her next instructions and
some advice. "Travel only at night. And don't set foot on the
road, ever." Then he wished her Godspeed. Harriet thanked
him and proceeded to follow the river northward.

Harriet walked all night to the next designated stop, this
time on the riverbank. Here, another stranger greeted her
calmly and kindly, just as the first two white people had at their
"stations." He helped her climb into his boat. He rowed for several miles, miles that Harriet would have had to walk had this
good man not been part of a network of kind Christian folks.

At the end of their journey, he sent her on foot to another
farm, where she was given a meal and a clever hiding spot
inside a big round bale of hay that sat in the middle of a field
full of such bales. Exhausted, she slept like a baby.

That night, the sky was overcast, and Harriet could not
see the North Star. She was slowed down by this, but not
stopped. She felt her way along in the dark from tree to tree,
feeling for the damp moss that grows only on the north side

and stumbling to the next tree. She managed to keep walking in the right direction.

Her next stop found her with a family of free blacks. For one entire week, they kept her in their cabin. She hid in a potato hole they had dug in their cabin floor. Harriet was grateful for having grown up on dirt floors. She liked the smell of the earth, and she felt no fear down there. They fixed the same kinds of foods Momma would have made, and it felt nice.

When the way seemed clear again, the black family sent Harriet on her way. She continued to sleep on the ground by day and travel by night.

The next stop was a farm owned by German immigrants, people known as Pennsylvania Dutch. Harriet loved the tidy barns they'd painted black and the swept-out livestock corrals. Even the farm animals were clean! Harriet enjoyed listening to the Germans speak in their own language, too. They hid her in their attic and fed her rich food. It tasted different than anything Harriet had ever eaten, but it was delicious and wholesome.

Her next stop was Philadelphia and freedom. It had taken time to travel and hide. She'd been the grateful recipient of hospitality from more strangers than she'd ever met before! Not once had she had a sleeping seizure, and she thanked God for that protection.

Now she was free! The thrill was indescribable. Her faith was strong. Not only had God seen her through, but He had shown her so many godly people in the world who were willing to risk their own lives for her. In spite of being far from home and family, Harriet's heart was lightened by such knowledge.

And Philadelphia was indeed a far cry from home. She'd never been in a city before, and Philadelphia was a big one. And it was cold! Harriet was a country woman, having grown up in a warm, humid part of the country listening to the soft sounds of birds and frogs and slave songs.

Now she heard horses clopping on the hard streets and people shouting all day long. Instead of smelling the sweetness in the damp air back home, here she smelled horse droppings and frying food. It didn't feel much like the Promised Land.

But it would do just fine. Harriet was free. She made herself adjust to the tall buildings and the fast, noisy way of life. She got jobs working in hotels and kitchens. She worked two and three jobs at a time, partly for the money, partly to stay busy.

And Harriet Tubman had a plan. She wanted to help other slaves. Running away had been dangerous, but it had been successful. Since arriving in Philadelphia, Harriet had met dozens of fugitive slaves. She came to know the organizations that helped them. She began to realize that to gain freedom, a slave needed courage, God's mercy, and the knowledge that it could be done.

Harriet also wanted her family with her. More importantly, she wanted every one of them to breathe freely, walk where they wished, and earn their own money. She wanted them to live with the amazing freedom she now had. If she could make it, they could, too! But they didn't know that. And they certainly didn't know how to go about it.

So Harriet determined that she would go back to Maryland as soon as she was able and spirit away her relatives. Maybe by now even John Tubman would change his mind and come with her. Her heart leaped at the thought.

One day, someone from the Underground Railroad mentioned that a free black man needed help to get his wife and two small children, who were slaves, north. The volunteers who helped fugitives in Philadelphia wanted a woman to help, since one child was a baby. Harriet listened, then recognized the names of her sister Mary and her husband.

"They're about to be sold," the volunteers explained. "Your brother-in-law thinks they can escape, but Mary needs help with the little ones. Do you know of anyone?"

"Me," said Harriet. "I'll do it."

The volunteers were adamant that she not be the one. Harriet was a fugitive from Maryland with a bounty price on her head. There was no way she should return to the South.

But Harriet laughed them off. "I'm not afraid. I understand how the Underground Railroad works, and I am the right person to bring them here."

And she was. A Quaker friend pretended to be a prospective slave buyer, and through a plan he had developed with Harriet's brave brother-in-law, Harriet's family was taken right off the slave auction block and hidden. They were able to escape to one station, on to another station, and then another.

Harriet waited for her family at a Quaker house in Baltimore. What a happy reunion! Then she confidently took them on the rest of the dangerous journey to Philadelphia.

One sister, and that sister's family were now free and with Harriet. She made plans to get more kin and anyone else who truly wanted to be free.

Now Harriet knew why the Lord had spoken to her loud

and clear. She decided to became a "conductor" for the Underground Railroad and devote her life to escorting slaves to freedom. That meant working and saving money for the journeys, staying close to the Fugitive Committee in Philadelphia, and eventually traveling to the South again.

Traveling to Southern states to bring more slaves to freedom was tremendously risky. It was just about the most dangerous thing Harriet could do. At any moment, she could be arrested as a fugitive slave. But Harriet knew God was on her side. And God made Harriet fearless.

In 1850, one year after Harriet had escaped to freedom, the Fugitive Slave Law was passed by Congress. This new law did two things. It made it a crime to help runaways anywhere in America, and it allowed former masters to reclaim runaway slaves even in the free Northern states.

Those slaves would then be returned to the South. This law agreed with Southern slave owners that slaves were the legal property of their masters and that such property should be returned.

The men in Congress fought for a long time over the Fugitive Slave Law. But in the end, they agreed to it, hoping it would prevent a war between the North and South.

Once passed, the new law made life dangerous for runaway black people in the North. They might be found by slavers from the South and returned to the plantations. Returned slaves were beaten harshly to teach them a lesson. Then they were often sold immediately. Their lives, which had been difficult before their journey north, would be much worse from then on.

Not only was the law dangerous to escaped slaves, but whites who helped them were outraged. Now they could be arrested and fined for helping runaway slaves in their own free states!

Since most of the sympathetic white folks who helped runaways did so because they believed they were fighting evil, they felt more anger than fear. They knew that, unlike their black brothers and sisters in Christ, they themselves would never be owned or whipped or sold. They also knew that this new law was immoral and had nothing to do with the laws of God or the love of Christ. So they felt no responsibility to obey it.

Stories began cropping up of whole communities defying the new law and rescuing captured slaves before they could be returned to the South. A few manhunters from the South were no match for a group of angry townspeople. Some slaves were spared in this way and sent on to Canada, where there was no such thing as a Fugitive Slave Law.

It was good to have some white folks on the slaves' side, but Harriet knew this law meant more trouble. Now there was no place in America where slaves could escape and live without looking over their shoulders all the time. She'd have to look into what could be done in Canada.

In the meantime, she continued her rescue work. Early in 1851, Harriet returned to her home county in Maryland to escort three slaves, one of them her brother, to Philadelphia. She went back again in the fall to the plantation owned by the doctor where she had lived. Harriet, dressed in a man's suit and hat, planned to persuade her beloved husband to come away with her.

Of course, Harriet had not seen or been in touch with her husband for two years. But she had dreamed of him constantly and truly believed he must miss her as much as she missed him. She was certain John would happily go north with her.

Harriet, who was otherwise so sensible and keenly observant of the world around her, seemed not to be able to see

John clearly. Even though he had threatened to betray her—an action that could have cost her her life—Harriet had a forgiving heart. She was still deeply in love with her husband. Time had passed. Surely he would be sorry he had been so stubborn and would want to come with her, his own wife.

One night, Harriet stood outside the cabin she had shared with John and knocked on the door.

"Someone's knocking, John," a voice said from inside. The voice belonged to someone unmistakably female.

John Tubman opened the door, looking as big and handsome as ever. Harriet stared up at him for a moment, speechless. Then she saw a beautiful young woman standing next to him. Harriet suddenly felt ugly and demeaned.

At first, John didn't recognize Harriet in her men's clothes. "Yes?" he said politely. Then he bent down and peered under her hat. "Harriet?" he said in a shocked voice. "Is that you?"

"This is Harriet?" the woman next to him said, disdain in her voice.

John began to laugh. "It sure is. Woman, what you doing dressed like that?" He laughed harder.

Harriet summoned up a smile. "I came back to take you with me, John."

"You what?" John stopped laughing for a moment. "I ain't heard from you in two years. Far as I knew, you were dead. Did you think I was just gonna wait for you?"

"But John—" Harriet began.

John interrupted her.

"You been out of the picture a long time now. You and me are over. I got me a new wife right here, Harriet. We jumped the broom together just last summer. My life is better than ever."

"But John—"

Harriet's protest was drowned out as John erupted into laughter. Then his new wife joined in. Without another word, Mr. and Mrs. John Tubman shut the door, leaving Harriet humiliated and alone in the dark.

Later in the woods, she thought things over. She felt such a wild bunch of emotions—love mixed with hate, sadness mixed with anger, awareness mixed with confusion. John was no longer hers. He had dismissed their marriage vows. He did not love her anymore.

As she mulled that over, Harriet realized that John had shown what he was made of back when she first spoke to him of escape. Clearly he hadn't loved her, even then. Wouldn't a husband want to protect his wife? Why had she thought he'd changed? How could she have risked her life—her entire mission—to come to him? He could still be a danger to her.

The worst thought of all for Harriet, though, was that part of her dream of freedom had included having John by her side. Now that dream had been killed by John himself. He could not have told her more clearly that he had no desire to be part of her life. He had taken another wife without even trying to find her.

Harriet cried softly in the woods. Then she slipped to her knees and prayed. After some time with the Lord, Harriet's wild emotions subsided to a dull ache. She knew the emptiness she was feeling inside would be with her for a long time. But for now, she had a mission. She was here in territory she knew. Surely there must be some slaves eager to escape.

There were. She gathered them that night, and together they made their way to Philadelphia.

With the effects of the Fugitive Slave Law making themselves seen, and with the death of her dream of married life with John, Harriet threw herself into her mission of freeing her family and anyone else who wanted to escape.

She continued to make trips to the South. She found ways to guide slaves out of Maryland without going with them by drawing maps on their cabins' dirt floors. She had them memorize the stops they would need to take. She only escorted the more difficult or complicated groups.

With this method, Harriet was able to help more slaves escape. Her instructions were so good and her routes so failsafe, nobody was ever caught. She gained a reputation. People called her Moses. When a throaty voice from someone who could not be seen started singing a soft rendition of "Go Down, Moses" in the quarters, people knew Harriet Tubman was around and willing to help them escape that very night.

Sometimes they heard a strong birdcall and realized that it wasn't the season for such birds to call. Then they knew Moses was around. The next morning, several slaves would be missing.

Harriet had gotten very good at making the journey north. Not only did she know the way and the stations well, she stayed in constant prayer so that her concentration was keen and her inner spirit alert to the suggestions of the Holy Spirit. This was especially important when she was being chased. It was frightening for runaways to hear the sounds of bloodhounds and horses, but Harriet would softly sing, "Wade in the water, wade in the water, children," to get the group into the river where their scent would be lost.

And sometimes she just knew things she should have had

no way of knowing. She'd find a way to keep her "passengers" safe.

Once going north, she sensed they were in immediate danger. She put everyone on a southbound train to throw their pursuers off their trail. After all, who would expect runaway slaves to be heading south? And on a train, no less.

She was creative, too. Wanting to spirit away more slaves from her former plantation, she once disguised herself as an old granny slave with a ragged dress and a scarf draped over her head to keep the sun off. She bought several live chickens, which she carried, then she slouched down like a doddering old woman and hobbled down the road in broad daylight.

Of all people, who should ride up the road on his horse but the doctor, her former master! Surely he would see the prominent scar on her face. Quickly, Harriet let go of the chickens so that they squawked and ran and half-flew every which way. Then waddling and bent over like an old woman, she chased after each one. The doctor watched for awhile, chuckling as he rode on.

Sometimes the very thing she worried over happened. She would have a seizure and fall into a deep sleep while trying to run slaves out of danger. But during this sleep, she had vivid dreams about what they should do and where they should go when she woke up. Harriet always obeyed these visions, even when they didn't seem to make sense. She believed they came from God.

Usually while on the run, Harriet and her passengers slept by day and traveled by night. But one morning as they were settling down to rest in the forest, one of Harriet's dreams told her they had to keep moving all day. The slavers were on their trail.

She woke everyone up and got them going again. Then she passed out in plain sight in the middle of a road. When she woke up, her passengers were waiting for her out there on that road, the sun shining down on all of them! Harriet was horrified that they could have been seen.

But they hadn't been seen, and Harriet's dream showed her that the bloodhounds were close. She ran everyone back into the woods and zigzagged in every direction until they reached a river. Even though she didn't know this particular river, it had been in her dream. And in the dream, she'd been shown that it had a sandbar on which they could cross.

The others were skeptical, but they had to trust Harriet. She started across the icy river, all five feet of her. Even though she waded up to her neck, the water never got any deeper. Sure enough, they got to the other side. Eventually they found themselves on an island where Harriet ran them through the woods until they came upon a cabin.

Would the inhabitants be friends or foes? Not to worry. Harriet had seen this in her dream, too. She knocked on the door, and a good Christian family of free blacks answered. There the runaways were able to rest and eat and dry their clothes by the fire.

The next day, they got back to the road by a different route. By noticing trampled grass, cigarette butts, and "Wanted" posters, they realized that the law had tracked them down right to the very spot where Harriet had passed out. The blood-hounds had indeed been on their trail, but the zigzagging had confused them. Then the scent of the runaways had been washed away in the river. The dogs could not find them.

Sometimes a slave was too frightened or too exhausted to

go on. But Harriet made that person go on for the sake of everyone else in the group. If even one slave turned back, the law would find ways to make that person talk. The entire Underground Railroad would be jeopardized for both black and white people. Black folks would be sent back to their masters, and white folks would be thrown into prison.

Because of this, Harriet always carried a gun. She prayed she would never have to use it, but when a slave threatened to turn back, she aimed the gun straight at the slave and said with absolute conviction in her voice: "Go free or die." The slave never turned back after that.

And God was merciful. In all her years as a conductor for the Underground Railroad, Harriet never pulled the trigger of her gun.

CHAPTER 8

As time went on, Harriet knew she needed to take her charges beyond Northern states and into Canada. Because of the Fugitive Slave Law and because Philadelphia was so often the stopping place for runaways, that city was no longer safe for escaped slaves.

Her first group of passengers to go to Canada started their journey just as winter hit. This trip took most of December to make, partly because there were eleven in the group. That was more people than Harriet had ever taken north at one time.

Since they were going farther and traveling during winter weather, it took longer than usual. It was not easy to keep such a large group going, fed, rested, and cheered.

For some time, the eleven fugitives hid with the great Frederick Douglass in cold and snowy Rochester, New York, near the Canadian border. Douglass was an escaped slave who was both educated and eloquent. He wrote letters and essays and made stirring speeches against slavery, which made him what was called an abolitionist. He and Harriet had tremendous respect for one another's work. He housed her large group for as long as it took to get money and provisions for them to pass safely into Canada.

Though much of the trip was on foot or by boat or wagon, during the last leg of the journey into Canada, the runaways were hidden in the baggage car of a train. Once the train crossed into Canada, the phenomenal Niagara Falls was in sight. And Niagara Falls meant they were in absolutely free territory.

Then the fugitives left the baggage car and sat in coach class, watching the mighty roaring waters and softly singing songs of thanks to God.

Harriet's group of eleven people headed toward the town of St. Catharines in Ontario, Canada. Many other ex-slaves lived there, enjoying not only free lives but full lives. They could even vote. Harriet began taking all her groups to St. Catharines, one group every spring, one group every fall.

In 1854, Harriet began having unnerving dreams about three of her brothers back in Maryland. She dreamed they were being sold to the chain gang. She knew what these dreams meant. Her brothers desperately needed to get out of Maryland. She prayed for a way to get a message to them that they must watch for her and come with her on her next journey.

Harriet remembered a free black man back in Maryland named Jacob who could read and write. Jacob knew Harriet's brothers. Jacob's adopted son lived in the North and sent letters to Jacob from time to time, so Harriet asked a friend to pen a letter to Jacob under the adopted son's name. She certainly couldn't use her own name, since she was wanted by the law in the South.

But secrecy was necessary for another reason. Local post-masters would open the mail of freed blacks. If there was something considered dangerous or illegal in a letter, Jacob could get in trouble.

The letter was worded carefully so that Jacob would understand that Harriet was coming to get her brothers. It read: "Tell my brothers to be always watching unto prayer, and when the good old ship of Zion comes along, to be ready to step on board." It was signed as if it were from Jacob's adopted son.

The postal authorities gave Jacob the letter and watched him read it. Jacob pretended to read it slowly and with much difficulty, though he'd read it quickly right away. Jacob knew his son had no brothers. There were other clues that told him the letter was not from his son but still intended for Jacob to read. He memorized its words, then told the postal authorities that he didn't understand a word of it and handed it back to them.

Jacob had already heard from a reliable source that Harriet's brothers were going to be sold with a lot of other slaves very soon. So he got to the brothers just as fast as he could to tell them that Harriet would be coming for them.

Harriet arrived in December. She got her group together and gathered supplies. Traveling north with her this time would be her brothers Benjamin, William Henry, and John. Also in this group were William Henry's fiancée, Jane Kane, who had dressed in a boy's clothes, and two nonrelatives, Peter Jackson and John Chase.

When it was time to leave, Harriet's brother John Ross was not to be found. "I'll leave word how he can find us," Harriet told the others. "We don't wait." She left word with Jacob, then she took her group to the plantation where her parents lived.

They spent Christmas Day hiding in the feed house near her parents' cabin where, blindfolded so that he could say he never saw his runaway children, Poppa Ross loaded them down with holiday food.

It was at the feed house where John Ross caught up with them, greatly agitated. He hadn't joined them earlier because his wife, Ann, had gone into labor. He wouldn't abandon her, and he ran for the midwife. Their child was born safely. John had left his wife and new baby, both of them crying. He knew that he would have been sold after Christmas anyway and separated from his family. At least this way he could promise his weeping wife that Harriet would come back for her next time.

The band of runaways made it safely north. And Harriet did return to bring back her sister-in-law, the baby, and another child of John and Ann's. When passengers were babies, Harriet would give them a small dose of paregoric, a drug people in the 1800s used as a painkiller. She knew how much to use to keep the baby sleeping but not harm it. Babies never slowed the journey down.

In 1857, Harriet determined that it was time to move her parents north. All her relatives had made it but them. And she'd been having disturbing dreams that those two old folks were about to be sold. In fact, her father was being interrogated almost daily by a plantation owner and the doctor for feeding a runaway. Since Poppa was clever, he was able to say honestly that he hadn't seen the runaway. (It had, after all, been a dark night when he'd fed him, and he had not been able to see him.) And since Poppa had a reputation for honesty, the doctor believed him. But who knew how long the doctor's trust would last?

Harriet's folks were old and arthritic. She knew they could not stand being separated from each other if they were sold. The time had come for action.

Harriet went south, journeyed to the plantation where her parents lived, and waited until dark to approach the cabin. Her parents were thrilled to see her. Poppa was still in trouble, and Momma was worried sick about it. Both of them moved so slowly. Harriet knew they could not escape on foot.

With her wisdom and daring, Harriet was able to find a horse and wagon. They loaded Momma's feather mattress in it, and off they went, traveling by night, sleeping in the wagon in the woods by day. Once they got out of Maryland and off the wagon, things got easier, and the trip to Canada was uneventful.

But Canadian weather was too extreme for the old folks. They were housebound in the winter and homesick, too. Harriet could see that they would not live long if she didn't provide a different home for them.

In spite of the Fugitive Slave Law and the fact that there was a high reward offered for her capture, Harriet moved her parents into New York. She doubted the bounty hunters would travel that far looking for two elderly slaves who could hardly walk. She bought them a house at 180 South Street in Auburn, New York, while she herself moved back to Canada. The winters in Auburn were rough, too, but they were milder than those in St. Catharines. Harriet continued to work to pay the mortgage on her parents' house and to bring more slaves to freedom.

During these years, Harriet began getting to know abolitionists in Boston. She also met John Brown, a compelling but disturbed white abolitionist who would later murder his way across the country in an attempt to free slaves. Harriet appreciated John Brown's insistence that slaves must be freed immediately, but she never agreed with using violence. So Harriet Tubman and John Brown never worked together.

But Harriet did, at the encouragement of other Northern abolitionists, begin speaking to groups about slavery. She told of the great risks slaves would take simply to be free, how they traveled under cover of darkness on foot with only the North Star to guide them. She spoke of her mission from the Lord. She relayed true stories of the Underground Railroad and was a compelling speaker with her deep and husky voice.

The fact that she sometimes lay right down and fell into deep sleep in the middle of a speech did not keep crowds from coming to hear her speak. When she'd wake up, she'd simply begin speaking from where she'd left off. Harriet became a popular speaker.

One day, she had a horrible intuition that something was wrong with John Brown. She could not shake the evil feeling. Later she learned that John Brown and his gang had seized a government arsenal at Harpers Ferry to help free slaves. In the standoff that ensued, many people were killed. John Brown survived, was put on trial, sentenced to death, and executed. Harriet wished violence had not been a part of John Brown's misguided plans for liberty.

The incident at Harpers Ferry was one of many that divided the opinions of the North and the South on the subject of slavery. Many in the North saw John Brown as a martyr. Many in the South felt even more threatened by their own slaves. Something tragic was bound to happen.

In 1861, the Civil War began, a bloody struggle between the Northern and Southern states of America. Much of what started this war was about the institution of slavery. The South needed slaves to continue its way of life. The North wanted the South to rid itself of slavery. Which side would win?

During the war, Harriet Tubman shifted her efforts. She worked with the Union Army in a fort under Union control in South Carolina. There she nursed sick, starving, and wounded slaves back to health. She searched the area for healing herbs and roots and brewed herbal medicines for them. She saved many lives in her role as nurse, and once again her charges called her Moses.

During this time, Harriet saw her first regiment of all black soldiers marching for the Union. It was a stunning sight. Black folks wept openly as the proud regiment marched by. Harriet quietly praised God that such a day had come, even if it was in a war.

Harriet also worked with the Union Army as a scout and a spy. Having brought slaves out of the South unseen all those years, she was perfectly prepared for such secretive work.

In 1863, she helped an army regiment of former slaves raid a Confederate camp and rescue about eight hundred slaves. They picked the slaves up in small boats and rowed them to huge gunboats, and Harriet sang the old songs to keep the slaves calm. This raid and Harriet's participation in it made front-page news in Boston. The Bostonians loved this courageous woman!

Harriet continued her hospital work for the army throughout the war. After the North claimed victory, the ratification of the Thirteenth Amendment brought an end to the painful era of slavery in the United States.

After Harriet Tubman escaped from slavery, she made nineteen more trips into the highly dangerous South. She was responsible for bringing three hundred slaves to freedom. Some were escorted by her. She gave others clear directions. But all of these slaves came face-to-face with the powerful and brave woman they called Moses who led man, woman, and child out of bondage with her throaty songs. As a conductor for the Underground Railroad, she never lost a passenger. They all arrived safely in the North.

During the Civil War raid, Harriet was responsible for rescuing about eight hundred more slaves. Nobody knows how many ex-slaves she saved by nursing them back to health in the camps through the war years.

In total, Harriet Tubman brought well over a thousand slaves to liberty. A true American, Harriet was chosen by God to lead her people to freedom. Not only did she perform these tasks at great personal risk, but she also gave up pleasures, comfort, and security in order to fulfill her mission. For many years, all her money and time were devoted to bringing slaves to freedom.

After the war, Harriet returned to her parents' house in Auburn, New York. There she worked to support her parents, and she continued her speaking engagements. She also spoke in favor of the rights of women, who at that time could not vote or own property.

In 1867, Harriet learned that John Tubman had been

murdered in Maryland. Harriet never married again, and she never had children, a rarity among women of the nineteenth century. She never made much money, and what she had, she gave to those in need, as Christ tells all Christians to do.

Harriet believed that when we open our homes to the poor, we entertain Christ Himself. So in her later years, she fed and housed poor black people in her home. Her house in Auburn, New York, was always open to the needy. She continued to raise money to help others.

In March 1913, Harriet Tubman died in Auburn and was buried in Fort Hill Cemetery. She is believed to have lived ninety-three years, but no one knows for sure when she was born.

In 1978, a postage stamp with her picture was released by the United States Post Office. The citizens of Auburn built Freedom Park, a tribute to Harriet's work in the cause of freedom.

Today, Harriet Tubman's house in Auburn is a museum about the Underground Railroad and Harriet Tubman. The house is owned and operated by the African Methodist Episcopal Zion Church. Tours are available.

Harriet Tubman is with the Lord now. But while she walked this earth, she devoted her life to what she felt the Lord would have her do.

CLARA BARTON

FOUNDER OF THE AMERICAN RED CROSS

by David R. Collins

CHAPTER 1

Snowflakes danced along the crust of the icy Massachusetts countryside on Christmas Day, 1821. Near the town of Oxford stood a quiet farmhouse. Excitement filled its kitchen.

"I do hope it's a girl!" ten-year-old Sally Barton squealed.

"Well, it's going to be a boy." David Barton winked at his brother Stephen.

"No, it's not," Sally protested. "Dorothy, tell them it's going to be a girl!"

As Dorothy, the oldest of the children, finished washing the last bowl, she handed it to Sally for drying.

"No one should care," Dorothy declared. "It's wonderful enough that it's happening on Christmas."

Wiping her hands, Dorothy sat in front of the fire. Sally, David, and Stephen joined her. Soon all four children were playing games before the crackling logs.

Suddenly, the door of the back bedroom opened. A tall, tired man came out and sat in a rocking chair.

"You've got a new sister," he announced.

"A girl—just like I said!" Sally twirled around the room.

Dorothy knelt beside her father. "Have you thought of a name?"

"Your mother and I decided to call her Clarissa Harlowe Barton."

"For Aunt Clarissa?" Stephen asked.

Father nodded.

David shook his head. "It's too long a name for a baby."

"Call her Clara if you like," Father answered.

Clara's early years passed quickly. Though the area had few children her age, she was never alone. While her brothers and sisters were at school, Clara followed her father around their farm.

Clara was her father's pet. Often he would set the dark-haired girl on his lap. Clara loved these times. She knew she would hear the old war stories. As a young man, her father had served his country bravely.

"Tell me again," Clara begged her father often. "Tell me everything you did."

Clara also loved animals. Button, their terrier, was Clara's favorite. They played together by the hour. Mama could never understand how they got so dirty.

Clara was a ball of energy. She begged her brothers and sisters to play with her when they came home from school. But after supper, she became a student.

Dorothy taught Clara to read. Teaching her to write was Sally's job. Math came from Stephen. Mother and Father taught her Bible verses.

Then there was David. "Enough of this book learnin'," he'd say. He showed her how to climb trees, pound nails, and run races. His lessons were always fun.

One day, as David and Clara sat on a fence near the meadow, a glistening black colt trotted up to them.

"I think he wants to take someone for a ride," David announced. He hoisted Clara to the colt's back. "Hold on to his mane, little one."

"David, I'm scared. What if I fall?"

"There's only one answer. Don't!" David ran to another

colt and jumped on his back. Giving the colt a quick clap on the back, he raced forward, slapping Clara's colt as he passed.

Away they galloped. Clara gripped the mane tightly.

"You're doing fine, Clara!" David cried. He led the way around the meadow several times, then returned to where they had started.

"Whoa!" he bellowed. Both horses jerked to a halt. David sprang down and ran to his sister. "You ride like a champion."

One night after the Bartons finished supper, David offered to wash dishes.

"Yes, Mama, we can finish these things," said Sally.

Mama shook her head. "There's something strange about all this help."

"Why, Mama," David began, "we just want to—"

"I know," Mama interrupted. "You just want something. Sally might volunteer to help, but you, David?"

"But—"

"Oh, let's ask her," Sally said. "Mama, we want to take Clara to school."

"What could a three-year-old girl learn at school?"

"She's almost four!" David exclaimed.

"She's much brighter than most of the children," a proud Sally added.

"Including me!" added David.

"Wait a minute!" Mama exclaimed. "You two are going too fast. A great deal of thought went into this performance."

"Well, we have talked about it," replied David. "You always say to have reasons for whatever you do."

Mama nodded. "And I also say that whatever you do must

make sense. Even if your father and I agree that Clara could go, how would she get there?"

"I could take her!" Stephen sprang up from his place on the hearth.

"Oh, another one is in on this plot. And what about your chores? Your father would never agree if chores were left undone."

"I'd just get up earlier," Stephen said.

Mama could see how badly her children wanted her to say yes.

"If your father agrees, it will be fine with me."

Instantly, she was swamped with hugs and kisses. Then the children dashed off to find their father.

"And where are my kitchen helpers now?" Mama asked herself.

The children found Father in the farmyard. He was harder to persuade. Finally he agreed.

On her first day of school, Clara was excited. Off she went, riding high on Stephen's shoulders. Sally and David, running ahead, paused now and then to throw snowballs at each other.

Suddenly, Clara looked very serious.

"Stephen, I'm frightened. I want to go home."

"Don't you want to learn things?"

"Yes, but I want to do it with you and Sally and everybody at home."

Stephen stopped and let her slip to the ground. He knelt on his knees before her.

"Clara, you learn things fast. You are ready for school. And you'll meet new friends."

"But won't people laugh at me? I want you to be proud of me."

"Clara, we are proud of you. We're glad you're going to school with us." He gave his sister a kiss. "Now let's hurry so we won't be late."

As she entered the schoolhouse, Clara was surprised at how crowded everything was. Seeing a seat in the corner, she ran to it and climbed up. David hurried over to her.

"Clara, you mustn't sit there. That's the dunce's chair."

"What's a dunce?"

"It's a student who doesn't know his lesson. If a student can't answer Colonel Stone's questions, the student must sit on this chair."

Clara jumped down. "I hope I never have to sit there, David. Have you ever had to?"

"Well. . .oh, there's Colonel Stone. You'd better sit up front so he can see you." Clara hurried to one of the front seats. She glanced back to make sure her brothers and sisters were still there. Seeing them gave her courage.

The first day at school slipped by quickly. In spelling, Clara surprised Mr. Stone by knowing third-grade words.

"How did your first day go at school?" Father asked at supper. "Did you have to sit in the dunce chair?"

"She climbed into it the moment she walked into the schoolhouse," David teased.

Clara's face turned red.

"At least, she'll never have to sit there because she doesn't know her lesson," Sally replied. "It seems to me that you did not know the third president of the United States, David Barton, and you had to sit—"

"Say, I think I'd better get some more wood for the fire." David grabbed his coat and hurried outside.

As the door slammed, Father roared with laughter. Soon everyone was laughing. And that night every Barton child recited the names of the presidents.

One night, Clara was the topic of conversation at supper. Everyone was concerned about her shyness.

"I think it would be best for Clara if she met more people and saw new places," Father said. "Maybe she should go to the Oxford boarding school. She would meet many children her own age."

"But, Father, I wouldn't be happy living anywhere else."

"How do you know, my dear? You've never been anywhere else."

Soon it was decided. Clara would go to boarding school in the spring.

Clara felt sad at the new school. She missed home. The more she tried to like the new school, the lonelier she became.

"Clara," her teacher said one day, "today's lesson is about the kings who ruled ancient Egypt."

"Yes, Sir."

"These kings made up a dynasty or line of royalty. Do you recall the name of this dynasty?"

Clara knew the answer.

"Pot-lemy," she stated proudly.

A loud laugh came from the back of the room. "Did you hear what she said? Potlemy!"

Soon the entire class was laughing. The teacher beat the narrow rod he was holding. "Quiet!"

Clara realized she had made a mistake. She had given the

right answer but pronounced it wrong. She buried her face in her hands.

The teacher walked to Clara and whispered that she could leave the room. Not stopping to gather her books, she ran out. She didn't stop until she reached her own room. Throwing herself on the bed, she cried herself to sleep.

Several days later, as she read a book, Clara heard soft tapping on the door.

"Come in," she called.

Her teacher opened the door and pulled up a chair next to the bed.

"Clara, you have visitors."

"Who?"

"Your father and brother. David, I believe."

"Oh, how wonderful. I can't wait to see them." She smiled brightly, but her teacher looked serious. "Is something wrong, Sir?"

"We decided it would be best for you to go home. We know you haven't been eating or sleeping well."

Clara hung her head. "I'm sorry. I like school, but I miss home so much."

"I know," he answered. "Now, you'd better get yourself packed up. That brother of yours looked as if he didn't like to be kept waiting."

"Now I know it's David." Clara jumped off the bed and threw her arms around her teacher. "I will miss you," she whispered.

An hour later, the Barton carriage was rolling homeward. Father held the reins as David told his sister of the move they had just made.

"You should see our new farm. Stephen and I found

several arrowheads near the gate."

"A new farm! I can hardly wait to see it."

"But there's work to be done," Father said. "Your mother will need help."

"Oh, I want to help. It will be fun!" Clara was bursting with excitement.

There was work to do. The farmhouse needed a coat of paint and many repairs. Although the farm was large, the Barton "family" had grown, too. Father had taken in some relatives and a boy.

Often Clara would climb Rocky Hill, where she could look out over the countryside. She wondered what she would become when she grew up. She could never make up her mind.

Then an accident helped her decide.

A barn was being raised on the Barton farm. Men from miles around came to work. The women fixed food. Clara's mother placed her in charge of pouring milk.

The morning passed quickly, and soon the men crowded in line for lunch. Clara poured glass after glass of milk.

At about three o'clock, Clara was finally able to sit down for a rest. She had just taken a sip of milk when she heard a loud scream. She ran toward the crowd.

"What happened?" No one answered. Clara pushed to the front of the crowd and looked up. Dangling from swaying ropes were two planks that had split in half. Directly below, men were helping a boy to his feet.

"David!" Clara rushed forward. "What happened to you?"

"Just. . .took a little tumble. Nothing to worry about."

David started to walk. He stumbled and was caught by two men.

"Are you all right, David?" Father stepped forward and examined his son's head. "That was quite a fall you took."

"I'm all right. Just let me rest a bit, and I'll be back on the job."

As the crowd broke up, Clara and Father helped David to a shady place.

"You're limping," Clara noticed.

"Now, don't you worry about me, Clara. I could race you to the river and beat you by a mile. You go mind the milk stand."

Clara had forgotten all about the milk. Several people were waiting in line.

"All right, but you rest."

"Yes, Mother." David gave his sister a wink.

But David was not all right. That night his head throbbed, and the next day he had a fever. The Bartons sent for a doctor.

By the time the doctor arrived, David's moans filled the house.

"David is a very sick young man," the doctor told the Bartons. "I tried to give him medicine, but he refused to take it."

Mama gasped. "What can we do?"

"Doctor, may I try giving him the medicine?" Clara asked.

"You?"

"This is his sister, Doctor. She and her brother are very close."

"I guess you can try." He handed the medicine to Clara. "Try to get him to take two spoonfuls."

Clara spoke to her brother in whispers. The loud moaning quieted. With a steady hand, she gave David the medicine. Then she left him to sleep.

"Help him get better, Lord," Clara whispered.

But the fever did not break.

As months passed, many doctors visited David. Each brought a different cure. None worked.

"I know he will get well," Clara said. "Just give him time. God will help him."

Each day she sat by David's bed and read to him.

Finally, a doctor came to take David away. Clara gathered up his things. Tears streamed down her face as she waved good-bye.

"Please, God," she whispered, "let David come back to us. Please."

Eventually, David became well enough to come home. Clara dashed from the house to greet him. Still pale, David hugged his sister with all his strength.

"Little one," he exclaimed, "you're the one who needs to become healthy. You're as tiny as a wart."

Together Clara and David regained their strength. Often they took the big family Bible and headed outside. Sitting in the shade, they shared the stories of Jesus.

"Just think," David said one afternoon, "Jesus could cure anyone."

"I love it when He brought Jairus's daughter back from the dead," Clara mused.

"You almost did that for me," David said. "I think you have a special talent for helping the sick."

Clara thought about David's words. Could the Lord mean for her to help sick people?

"Please give direction to my life," Clara prayed often. "And give me strength to do Your will."

CHAPTER 2

Clara sat on the sofa, buried beneath a mound of blankets. "Mumps!" she muttered. "What a way to be sick." She hated being sick, especially with company in the house.

Clara could hear her parents talking with their guest Mr. Fowler, a famous lecturer. Suddenly she heard her name.

"You have a very interesting daughter in Miss Clara," Mr. Fowler said. "Her features show great strength."

"True, Mr. Fowler," agreed Mama. "But she is so shy. She loves people yet is timid with them."

"Give her some responsibilities. She would be a perfect teacher."

The Bartons wasted no time in taking his advice. Soon it was arranged for Clara to teach in the nearby District 9 schoolhouse.

On a crisp spring morning, fifteen-year-old Clara marched up the pathway to her new school. She opened the door of the one-room building and was greeted by a loud chorus.

"Good morning, Miss Barton."

Before her were forty faces. Making her way between the wooden benches, Clara walked to the teacher's desk. Picking up a Bible, she announced that the class would read a few verses.

As the children read, Clara felt wonderful. Her students wanted to learn, and she would guide them.

When recess came, the children scrambled outside. Then trouble arrived.

"Miss Barton! The big boys won't let us play with our ball," cried a little girl, her clothes covered with dust.

"Doesn't every grade have a ball?"

"Yes, Miss Barton. But the boys take them. When I tried to get ours back, they pushed me."

Clara strode out to the playground. Four tall boys held the balls.

"I understand we have a problem. These balls must be shared."

"There ain't no misunderstandin', Teacher. We're sharin'. See? Bill's got two; George's got three; Henry's got—"

"Each grade is to have one ball. Now, why don't you boys—"

"Teacher, why don't you let us get back to our game?" Turning his back, the boy heaved a ball toward a barrel forty yards away. The ball fell about two feet short.

"What's the matter? Can't you throw that far?" Clara asked.

The boy flashed her an angry look, then threw again. The ball passed the barrel by several feet.

"Too bad! You should practice more."

"All right, Teacher. Show me how." The boy tossed a ball to Clara.

Clara knew she had to hit her target. *Lord, help me,* she prayed. Blocking the sun with her free hand, she thrust the ball straight ahead.

All eyes watched the ball whiz through the air. It dropped into the barrel. The small children erupted in cheers.

Clara turned to the four boys. "Shall we return to the classroom? We might find something for you to read on the subject of throwing—and something else on the subject of manners."

She turned and marched triumphantly to the school. "Thank You, Lord," she whispered.

In the months that followed, Clara became known as a good teacher. The older boys admired her for her strength and agility. The younger children loved to hear her stories.

On the final day, Clara thanked her students for their help. As they left, each child handed her a small present. When the schoolhouse was empty, Clara noticed an envelope on top of the gifts. Opening it, she found a slightly smudged sign: To the Champion Teacher.

She looked toward the door and saw four smiling boys peeking in.

Teaching gave Clara confidence. Job offers flowed in. For once, new places did not frighten her.

While Clara taught, David and Stephen became owners of several lumber factories. During the summer, Clara helped them. She suggested forming a school for children of the factory workers.

"They need a school," she pleaded. "Can't you find me a patch of space for a classroom?"

Stephen and David offered her an unused packing room. The first day of school brought seventy children, one tame crow, and two pet goats. Clara persuaded her brothers to build a real school. Soon there were 125 children.

For ten years, Clara taught. Finally, Clara decided she ought to go back to school.

In 1850, Clara entered the Liberal Institute in Clinton, New York. She became close friends with another student, Mary Norton.

After graduating, Clara paid Mary a visit in New Jersey.

The Nortons treated Clara as one of the family, and she enjoyed herself. But one thing bothered her.

"Mary, why are children roaming the streets?" As the two women shopped, they were constantly shoved by young boys.

"Why don't you ask one of them?" Mary answered.

"I will." Clara caught the collar of one of the boys running by. "Why aren't you in school?" she asked.

"Who's got money for school, Lady?" The boy darted away.

"What did he mean by that, Mary?"

"Well, Bordentown schools are private. You have to pay to attend. We don't have schools that are open for everyone."

"Well, it's time you did have open schools. Whom can I talk to about this matter?"

"Mr. Suydam is head of the school board," Mary said.

"Where is he?"

"About two doorways straight ahead. He's the postmaster, too."

Clara sped toward the post office. Behind the counter stood a bearded man.

"May I help you ladies?"

"Yes, you may," Clara said. "And you might also help the young people in this town."

The old man was startled. Few women spoke so forcefully.

"I want to know why children are running all over the streets of this town," Clara continued. "I want to know why they aren't in school. I want to know why—"

"Please! I don't know your name, young lady, but—"

"My name isn't important, but my questions are. You are the head of the school board?"

The man nodded.

"Are you aware that a New Jersey law says each child must receive a free education?"

"Yes, but we have several private schools in the area which take care—"

"Of those students who can afford to go. Isn't that correct?"

"Well, there is a tuition fee, though I don't see—"

"Then a New Jersey law is not being enforced in this town."

"But no one has ever suggested we have free school. All the people—"

"It has now been suggested! How many youngsters attend your private schools?"

"About two hundred—eight more than last year." Mr. Suydam beamed in pride.

"And how many youngsters in this town are not attending school?"

"I, well, I. . .guess there might be about four hundred."

"Those figures show that a new school is needed. I offer my services as a teacher."

"But the school budget doesn't call for—"

"There is no need for a salary at this point, Mr. Suydam. May I count on your help?"

The man was stunned. "I suppose—"

"Good, we'll start making plans immediately." Clara turned and marched out the door.

She got her school. In three years, attendance rose from six to six hundred. Eventually, Clara's health gave way. She lost her voice completely, and her doctors ordered her to take a long rest.

Returning home from town one afternoon, Clara overheard a group of people talking.

"It sure doesn't look good in Washington. I hate to think what's going to happen," a man said.

"Sure looks like a war's shapin' up," another grumbled.

Clara could not sleep that night. She tossed and turned. She prayed. Suddenly she sat up and lit a candle.

"I'm going to Washington!" she announced. "I might be needed there."

Clara stood before the mirror and smoothed her dress. This was her first day at a new job.

On top of her bureau lay a letter from Congressman Alexander DeWitt, a family friend. When she'd decided to go to Washington, Clara had written Mr. DeWitt. He found Clara a job with the United States Patent Office.

Clara gave her room one last look. Stuffing a lace handkerchief into her handbag, she closed and locked the door.

Washington was an exciting city. More than forty thousand people lived in the nation's capital. Visitors streamed into the city from all over the world.

Yet there was a strange feeling. Men huddled together and spoke in whispers. Clara wondered if they were discussing war.

Clara was not welcomed by everyone when she arrived at the patent office. Some men blew smoke in her face. A few spit tobacco juice at her feet.

Mr. Mason, the man who had hired Clara, met her with a smile. He asked her into his office. She seated herself in an overstuffed chair.

"Mr. Mason, many of your workers are not happy about my presence here."

"Well, Miss Barton, I'm afraid that some of our men will not treat you pleasantly."

"Have I done something to offend them?"

"Of course not. But you are the first woman clerk in Washington. Men have always held clerks' jobs."

"It seems to me that a position should be held by the person who can do it best."

"My feelings as well, Miss Barton. But some people disagree. You will probably receive some rude treatment for awhile."

"I appreciate your help, Mr. Mason." Clara stood. "Now, may I see where I'm to work? I'd best start proving my worth."

"Certainly, Miss Barton."

Clara was led to a large table piled with books and papers. It was difficult to ignore the sneers of the clerks, but Clara reminded herself of Jesus' words: "Love your enemies."

"You will copy the information on these records into these books," Mr. Mason explained. "Mr. DeWitt said your writing is very neat. You'll certainly be able to display your talent here." Mr. Mason smiled and excused himself.

Clara's job was tiring. Her fingers grew sore, and her back ached. She missed her family and friends. Sometimes Clara spent her free time listening to speeches in the United States Senate.

"Each state should decide for itself whether slavery is legal," declared Southern senators.

Northern senators disagreed.

When President James Buchanan was elected in 1856 to replace President Pierce, Clara lost her job and went home to Massachusetts. Soon she received a letter from the patent office.

"We have been unable to secure a competent replacement for you," the letter read. "Please consider returning."

Clara traveled back to Washington. She found an uneasy city. Crowds gathered at street corners. Angry speakers shouted at people walking by.

In November 1860, Abraham Lincoln was elected president. Immediately, seven Southern states agreed to withdraw from the United States. They elected their own president.

In Washington, Clara received an invitation to attend the Inaugural Ball in honor of President Lincoln. The morning of March 4, 1861, was brisk. Clara bundled herself well and walked to the Capitol. She listened to Abraham Lincoln take the oath of office. After his speech, Clara hurried home. By afternoon, she was sick.

"I will be unable to attend the ball," she wrote to a friend that night. "It is a sad disappointment to me. But I only pray that President Lincoln can find a way to pull the country together. The talk of war is everywhere. Voices are loud and angry. I am reminded of an old saying from Proverbs—'A soft answer turneth away wrath.' There seem to be no soft answers anymore, only bitter and noisy argument. Surely our actions cannot please God."

CHAPTER 3

"The South opened fire on Fort Sumter."

Clara could not believe her ears as she hurried to work one April morning in 1861.

Soon young soldiers flooded the city.

One day, Clara stood on the platform at the Washington train station. In a few minutes, a train would steam in bearing soldiers from her hometown in Massachusetts.

As the train pulled in, Clara smiled and waved.

"Hey, there's Miss Barton!" a voice shouted.

Soon Clara was surrounded by friends and former students.

In the weeks that followed, Clara made frequent trips to the capital to visit the soldiers. The Massachusetts regiments were housed in the Senate chambers. Clara tore up sheets and wrapped them into rolls of bandages for the soldiers. She sewed up ragged uniforms. Sometimes she baked delicious pies.

Wounded soldiers were brought to the Capitol lawn because there was no better place to take them. As Clara walked to the Senate chambers one morning, she noticed a soldier sleeping on the lawn. A large wound on his head looked badly infected. Clara strode to one of the doctors nearby.

"Sir, I believe you have a patient with a severe wound that has not been attended to. Do you suppose—"

"Do you suppose you might just go about your own business and leave us alone?" the doctor snapped.

"But this boy's wound is infected. He needs help right

away. If he doesn't—"

"They all need help right away. Now, if you don't mind, I have other things to do."

"But I do mind!" Clara said. "If that boy had received proper treatment, he would not be in the condition he is in now."

"If he had received proper treatment at the battlefield, he would probably be recovered by now."

"Then why didn't he?" Clara asked.

"No one is there. Now, if you will excuse me, I have several things to take care of."

The doctor walked away, leaving Clara gazing at hundreds of wounded soldiers.

"Someone should be there when these boys are shot. I'm going to find out why they aren't."

The supply wagon came to a jerky halt as Clara tugged on the reins. It was almost midnight, and she had been traveling since daybreak.

Clara stepped down from the wagon and looked around. No one was nearby. Wearily, she climbed the stairs to a building and entered.

Once inside, Clara could hear the moans of wounded men. A candle moved. Clara walked toward it, being careful not to fall over any of the injured soldiers on the floor.

A man was carrying the candle. His doctor's jacket was dirty.

"Sir. . .Sir."

The doctor turned. "What are you doing here?" He was not happy.

"I've come to help."

"You've come to help! And what can you do? Sweep the floor?" He turned abruptly and moved to another soldier.

Clara turned to leave, but then she stopped. Hadn't she worked for days collecting supplies? Weren't there hundreds of men in this room who needed help? *I need Your strength,* Clara prayed.

She walked back to the doctor. "I have come a long way to help," she said quietly. "I have things in my wagon which I think you can use."

"And what are these things? Cookies? Cakes? Young lady, I'm sure you mean well by coming here, but I'm afraid—"

"I am not speaking of cookies," Clara interrupted. "I am speaking of medicine, bandages, shirts, socks."

"Are you telling the truth?"

"If you follow me, you will see that I am." Clara marched outside. The doctor followed eagerly. He climbed into the wagon.

"I can't believe it. How did you get these things? Who are you? Where did you come from?"

"Later on, we can talk. Right now, we had best unload these things."

"Yes, yes!"

The two worked through the night.

"Some of these things should be taken into Culpepper," the doctor said the next morning. "I'll get a man to take them."

"I'll do it. I'm the only one who knows what things are in which boxes."

"But you're tired. Don't you wish to rest?" the doctor asked.

"That will come later. May I go?"

"Well, if you wish, Miss. Say, I don't even know your name."

"Miss Barton, Sir. Clara Barton."

"And I am Dr. Dunne. James Dunne. I'm pleased to meet you, Miss Barton. I apologize for my lack of manners earlier."

"That's quite all right, Sir. Now, may I go?"

"Certainly."

Clara and Dr. Dunne loaded several boxes of medicine and clothing back into the wagon. Soon Clara was headed down the road.

The tiny town of Culpepper lay in ruins. Clara stopped her wagon. "Could you tell me where I might find the military hospital?" she asked a man.

"You mean hospitals, don't you, Miss? Any of these buildings."

"All these buildings are hospitals?" Clara's voice showed her surprise.

"Yup. There's Yankees and Rebs in every one."

Shocked, Clara climbed down and entered the nearest building. Everywhere she looked there were injured soldiers.

Wasting no time, Clara began unloading supplies. She was soon helped by several doctors. Word spread through the hospital of her arrival. Soldiers greeted her joyfully.

The next few weeks were busy. Clara applied new bandages, gave medicine, cooked meals, and wrote letters for the men.

One day bad news arrived. "General Jackson has attacked at Bull Run. Sounds like a slaughter."

A doctor arranged for Clara to go by train to the battlefield.

Loading supplies into a boxcar, Clara stopped to wipe her forehead. Suddenly, she heard a chant coming from the Culpepper hospitals. She could just make out the soldiers' words.

"Thank you, Miss Barton. God bless you."

Clara was happy to have helped the men. But the job had just begun.

The train ride was bumpy. Clara did her best to keep the stacks of supplies from falling over. After traveling all night, the train pulled into a tiny railroad station. Clara jumped up and climbed out of the train.

Wounded soldiers covered the ground as far as she could see. A chain of wagons stretched along the road to the horizon. Each wagon was crowded with soldiers moaning in pain.

"Begging your pardon, Ma'am." A young soldier clutched at Clara's arm. She turned just in time to catch him as he fell. Clara eased him to the ground. He had been shot in the chest.

"Ma'am, are you Miss Barton?"

"Yes, Son. Now lie quietly, and we'll take care of you." Clara wiped the boy's head with her apron. "Quickly," she called to a nearby soldier, "bring me that small brown bag from the boxcar."

"I'm afraid it's too late for that, Miss Barton. But would you do me a favor? My name's Harvey Johnstone. Would you tell my folks good-bye? They're staying just outside Washington with some people named Clarke. I'd be greatly indebted to you if—"

The boy died in Clara's arms. Her eyes filled with tears.

"Here's your bag, Ma'am."

Clara took the bag from the soldier. Pulling a piece of paper from it, she scribbled down the boy's name and wrote the name

Clarke beside it. Then she shoved it back into the bag.

"Miss Barton, should we start unloading?"

"Yes, of course. From the look of things, I'd say these men need food."

In minutes, Clara was cooking huge kettles of stew. The smell of food brought smiles to many soldiers.

Next, Clara tried to make the wounded more comfortable. Bales of hay were scattered on the ground to make softer beds.

Then Clara began cleaning and dressing wounds. When evening arrived, it grew cold. She worried about men getting pneumonia. She walked up and down rows of the injured, making sure they were covered with quilts or blankets.

As she knelt beside one man, she noticed a light growing larger several yards away. A small fire had started from a candle being tipped over. She threw down the nearest quilt and smothered the fire.

For the rest of the night, Clara watched for fires.

Dawn was a welcome sight. Clara busied herself boiling hot coffee.

Suddenly, a Union scout raced into camp.

"They're coming. The Confederate cavalry. They're just over that hill."

A chill raced through Clara. How could the hundreds of wounded men be moved?

Soon the wagons were being loaded with the injured. Clara made sure each wagon had some food.

"Miss Barton, you'd best leave this area. The danger is very great." A Union officer looked worried as he spoke.

"I can't leave now. There are men to be cared for."

"But you may be captured, Miss Barton."

"And you might be too, Sir. But you are not leaving."

"These are my men. It's my job to see that they are kept safe."

"Then I suggest we load them faster." Clara flashed a smile.

By midafternoon, heavy drizzle covered the area. Men were being loaded onto trains. Cannon fire came closer.

Finally, all the injured were loaded. Clara was pulled into a boxcar. She took a final look at the muddy scene.

As the train chugged its way down the tracks, a soldier shouted that Confederates were attacking the camp. Clara stared sadly out into the night.

CHAPTER 4

"Miss Barton, let me help you."

A huge Union soldier helped Clara up into an army wagon.

"Thank you. I'm afraid I wouldn't have been able to make it myself."

"From what I hear, you're able to do just about everything. Giddyap, you long-eared mulies!"

The army wagon surged forward on the Washington road. The driver often waved to people.

"Do you know all those people you're waving at?" Clara asked.

"Nope, but its kinda fun to pretend."

Clara smiled. She was going to like her new driver. "Can the wagon move any faster?" she asked.

"Sure can, Miss Barton. Hold on." The driver snapped the whip above the mules' heads, and the wagon rolled rapidly out of the city.

"How far is it to Harpers Ferry?"

" 'Bout eighty miles, Miss Barton. But this road will make it seem like eight hundred. More bumps on it than on a toad's back."

The wagon bounced all over the road, but Pete drove with a careful hand.

"I hear that battle at Chantilly was a terrible mess," Pete said. "Heard you almost got caught by those Rebs."

Clara nodded. Chantilly had been terrible. General Lee sent his troops to destroy the small town in Virginia. By the time Clara had arrived, the town was ruined. Hundreds lay injured. When the Confederates swooped down for a final attack, she'd escaped on horseback.

"Say, look up ahead!" Pete slowed the horses.

Hundreds of wagons crawled along the road as far as they could see.

"Isn't there something we can do, Pete? We will never get to Harpers Ferry behind this mess."

"Nuthin' much we can do, Miss Barton. The road's too narrow for passing. Looks like those wagons up front are pullin' off for the night. Guess we might as well, too."

The wagon creaked to the side of the road. Clara climbed down and began cooking supper.

After eating, Clara took a walk. Wounded soldiers were scattered by the road. She helped whenever she could. Suddenly she had an idea. Hurrying back to the wagon, she jostled Pete out of his sleep.

"Pete, we can go now!"

Pete rolled over and sat up.

"Who. . .what. . .what's happened?" he asked.

"It's time to go," Clara exclaimed. "Look! The moon is full, and the road is bare. We can travel tonight and pass all these wagons."

Pete was finally awake. He stared at Clara.

"But we need rest. Now, why don't you crawl into the wagon and get—"

Clara stared at him. "If you won't drive this wagon, I will."

Pete scratched his head. "Well, my orders are to take you where you want to go. I guess that means when, too."

Clara quickly loaded the things they had used for cooking.

Pete lined up the mules, and soon the lonely wagon was rolling over the road. The next morning, it had passed hundreds of wagons and was near the head of the train.

By noon, Clara was in Harpers Ferry. She quickly took charge of the injured.

The next morning, excitement filled Harpers Ferry. News had drifted in that Confederate and Union troops were preparing to clash about ten miles away.

"The battle will take place on Antietam Creek. That's right near Sharpsburg, Maryland." The soldier spreading the news was shaking. "Generals Lee and Jackson are lining up their soldiers. Gonna fight McClellan, Burnside, and Hooker. What a battle!"

In no time, Clara loaded a wagon. By afternoon, she was at a farmhouse-hospital. Cannons exploded nearby. As Clara jumped down from the wagon, a welcome face greeted her.

"Dr. Dunne, how good to see you again!"

"And how wonderful to see you, Clara. I've heard so much about you since our first meeting. We must have a long talk."

"Yes, but let's get my wagon unloaded."

"I won't ask if you brought cookies." Dr. Dunne's eyes twinkled.

Clara and Dr. Dunne worked long hours. The farmhouse was flooded with injured soldiers.

"I don't understand this war," Dr. Dunne burst out one day. "Some of these boys are fighting members of their own family."

Clara knelt to give a Union soldier a drink of water. She, too, could not understand the war.

Crack! A bullet tore through the sleeve of Clara's dress.

The bullet hit the soldier. He lay dead.

After a moment, Clara stood up and walked to the next injured man. The living had to be helped.

As the battle at Antietam went on, cannon fire came closer to the farmhouse. At times, everything would shake. Finally came the news Clara had feared.

"Miss Barton, there's no food. What'll we do?"

Clara tried to think of something. "How about the medicine we brought along to treat snakebite? What's it packed in?"

"I'll go see."

The soldier disappeared into the cellar. He soon returned with three wooden cases. He pried them open and began uncovering the bottles of medicine.

"Hallelujah!" he exclaimed.

Clara came running. "What is it?"

"Look, Miss Barton!"

Clara took a handful of soft yellow powder from one of the cases. "Cornmeal!"

"Miss Barton, it's like a miracle!"

"Well, let's use this miracle. Get a fire set up outside. We'll make the biggest batch of cornmeal gruel you've ever seen. Somebody go down into the cellar and see if there are any kettles."

Two soldiers sprang to their feet and ran down the cellar stairs. "Miss Barton! Come down here!"

Clara hurried into the cellar.

"Look, Miss Barton. Three bags of flour and a whole bag of salt. Must have been stored here for years. Can we use 'em?"

"Of course. We'll make hardtack. These men will have a feast."

“Why, yes. How did you know?”

“Top secret, Miss Barton.” The general winked. “You are far more famous than you realize.”

"General Rucker, I'm not interested in being famous. I'm interested in this report. We lost so many lives. Isn't there any hope of this war ending?"

"Miss Barton, there is always hope."

Clara rose from her seat. She walked to the window. "It's so sad to see young boys going to war. Many never go home."

She returned to the desk. "Where may I go that I will be most needed?"

General Rucker pulled out a map. He pointed to a small dot by a crooked line.

"This is Fredericksburg, and this is the Rappahannock River. There's a deserted mansion called the Lacy House right about here."

"I shall leave in the morning." Clara tied her bonnet and walked to the door. "Oh, General Rucker, may I have three wagons for this trip? The last time—"

"No, you may not have three wagons!" General Rucker's eyes twinkled. "You shall have six wagons and an ambulance."

"Thank you," Clara whispered.

The Lacy mansion, with its twelve rooms, stood empty under a heavy blanket of snow. Clara shivered as she carried her lantern through the lonely house. Each room was ready for the task ahead.

Walking out to the patio, Clara looked down the hill. Below her lay the river. Nearby, Union campfires glowed. Across the river, the Confederates held Fredericksburg. There was no bridge. The Union soldiers would build one. It would not be easy.

Early the next morning, Clara awakened to the shouts of men. Rushing to her window, she saw Union soldiers working on a bridge. By afternoon, the first attack was under way.

A cannon bellowed from the opposite shore. Soldiers crossing the bridge were thrown into the water and carried downstream.

More cannons blasted. The Lacy mansion shook from the explosions. The front door flew open.

"Here come the injured!" a lieutenant called.

Clara raced to the door. Stretcher after stretcher was being carried up the yard.

The rooms were soon packed with Union soldiers. They were on the staircase, in the cellar—anyplace they might be safe.

"Our men are in Fredericksburg!" The news roared through the house. Clara looked out the window and could see a line of blue uniforms crossing the bridge.

A redheaded boy ran up to her. He stuffed a note into her hand: *Come to me. Your place is here.*

"Where did you come from?" she asked the boy.

"Fredericksburg. The doctor there said to get you."

"I'll have to gather supplies. Here, keep this bag open and follow me." Clara stuffed the bag with medicine.

One of the doctors tried to stop her. "You can't make it over that bridge. We've already lost hundreds of soldiers."

Clara wouldn't listen. Scrambling over the bridge, she heard a shot whistle past. It seemed to take hours to get across. Reaching the opposite shore, Clara stumbled up the hill. The boy caught up with her and led her into Fredericksburg.

A Union officer rode up. "You're in great danger, Ma'am. Do you want protection?" he asked.

"Thank you, General. But I believe I'm the best-protected

woman in the country. I have the entire army as my guard."

Some soldiers overheard her. They cheered wildly. "Hooray for the Union! Hooray for Miss Barton!"

The general smiled down. "Ma'am, I believe you are right."

Clara entered a shattered wooden building filled with injured men.

"Clara! Clara Barton!"

"Dr. Cutter!" Clara went up to the old surgeon.

"I knew you'd come, Clara. I hated to call on you, but we need you so badly."

Clara smiled at the doctor. He was a member of the Massachusetts Twenty-first Regiment. Her regiment.

"Clara, we have our hands full. The wounded keep pouring in. We'll have to get them back across the river. I heard you have the old Lacy mansion."

"Yes, it was filling fast when I left. But if these boys must be moved, we will find room for them."

Clara and Dr. Cutter started moving the injured. Soon Lacy House bulged with twelve hundred wounded men. They shivered in the cold December air. But each face lit up as the tiny woman they knew and loved came near.

Christmas night, as Clara stared out her window, a light snow began falling. She thought of Christmases in the little farmhouse in Oxford. She thought of her family.

Loud singing broke out. Clara flung open her door. She stood speechless as a crowd of men sang: "Happy birthday, Miss Barton. Happy birthday to you."

"How did you know?"

The only answer she received was the smiling faces of her patients.

When the injured had been cared for, Clara went back to Washington for more supplies. She pulled her cape close as she stepped off the streetcar near her home.

Clara unlocked the door of her room and stumbled in. Lighting a candle, she noticed a box on her bed. Her name was written on it.

Clara cut through the cord around the box. A small card fell to the floor. Clara picked it up. *From your friends in Oxford and Worcester,* she read.

Clara was amazed. The box was full of shoes, gloves, shirts, collars, and a dress! She held up the lovely green silk and whirled around the room. Her tired body came alive.

In a few weeks, Clara had a chance to show off her new dress. She received a note to go to Ward 17 of Lincoln Hospital.

Why do they want me there? she wondered. She put on her new dress and hurried off.

As she walked through the door, a great cheer arose. Before her stood seventy men, injured soldiers from the Battle of Fredericksburg. They saluted her.

"I don't know what to say," she gasped. "It is all so wonderful!"

"And so are you, Miss Barton!" the men shouted. "You're the best soldier in the country!"

CHAPTER 5

A kitten tangled itself in long strands of yarn. Clara looked down from her darning and chuckled.

"See what you've done. How will we ever get you loose?" She lifted the kitten into her lap and pulled the yarn away.

"I shall miss you while I'm gone." The kitten had been a present from the Speaker of the House of Representatives, Schuyler Colfax. But there was no place for a tiny pet on the battlefront. Clara was preparing to leave Washington for South Carolina. The Union Navy was going to attack Charleston.

By afternoon, supplies were loaded on the *Aragon,* a small transport ship. Clara took her kitten to a neighbor. Soon she was sailing toward the wooded hills of the Carolinas.

Clara had become known as the Angel of the Battlefield, and soldiers cheered as she entered the harbor.

"I don't deserve this praise," she protested. "Many others have done far more than I." Nothing she said could stop the cheers.

Before long, Clara was in action. Union ships bombarded the Charleston harbor. Ship after ship returned, filled with wounded soldiers.

Clara moved the place for treatment to the islands outside Charleston. Now she could take care of the wounded more quickly.

The summer of 1863 brought new troubles. Whirling sand covered food and medicine. Insects attacked supplies. A scorching heat wave brought deadly fever.

"I must order you to go," Clara was told. "You are pale and look tired. I cannot risk having you stay. You should probably be in one of your own hospital beds."

"I'm all right," Clara insisted, and she stayed.

But Clara was wrong. In October, she collapsed. She lay in bed for weeks, unable to move. One day, she awoke to find a welcome visitor.

"David, is it really you?"

"Yes, Clara. It's your old brother, David."

Clara smiled. "Oh, David, I have to get out of this foolish bed. There's so much to do."

"Now listen, little one. The only thing that needs to be done right now is for you to get better. You came very near leaving us. It's time you rested."

"But David, what of the war? The soldiers?"

"And what of you? If you will not think of yourself, I shall have to. You are going to take a rest."

Clara followed her brother's orders. She boarded the *Aragon* and headed for Washington. From there she returned to Oxford and spent several weeks visiting friends. But the memories of injured soldiers drew her back to the battlefield. "Lord, give me the strength I need," she prayed.

The call came from Fredericksburg. Thousands of soldiers lay injured. More than two thousand were dead.

Rain poured over Washington as Clara boarded a steamer early in May 1864. The crowded boat would take her down the Potomac. From Belle Plain Landing, she would go ten miles by wagon to Fredericksburg.

"You'd better get inside and find yourself a seat, Lady," a deckhand called to her.

"Thank you," Clara answered. "Do you think this rain will stop soon?"

"Nope, and it's likely to be an awful muddy mess at Belle Plain."

He was right. As the boat steamed into the dock, Clara saw wagons stuck in mounds of mud.

"See what I mean?" the deckhand asked Clara. "Those wagons are full of our boys. Just no way to get 'em aboard."

"There has to be a way!" Clara snapped. She picked up her baskets and walked down the plank to the shore. She sank to her knees in mud.

"Can I help you, Ma'am?" A young man offered his hand to Clara, and she took it gratefully.

"I'm afraid the men in the wagons need your help more than I," she said.

"We're doin' all we can for them. Are you from the Christian Commission?"

"No, but I'd be glad to help you if I can," Clara replied.

"We'd like to get these men fed. We've got some food—mostly crackers—and if we can find a place to heat some coffee. . ."

"There's a place." Clara rushed forward. "By that stump over there. See if you can gather up some brushwood. I'll get some kettles ready."

The kettles soon sizzled with boiling coffee.

"The men will be glad to get this," Clara's new friend said. "I only wish we had a way to take these crackers to them." He pointed to a large barrel.

"We can manage it quite easily." Clara pulled two linen scarves from her baskets. She flipped them open in the air.

"Turn around," she ordered.

As the man turned, Clara tied one of the scarves around his waist.

"Never had an apron on before," he muttered.

"Well, this is a good time for it. Put some crackers onto your lap and fold the apron over them. Then tie it in, like this." Clara demonstrated with her own scarf.

"Say, that's clever. Have you been at any other battles?" the man asked.

"A few. Have you?"

"No, this is my first. I signed up for the Christian Commission. Want to do my part. Sure glad you came along."

"You'd have done all right," Clara said.

"Well, I'd best get some of this coffee delivered—and the crackers, too." He patted his apron and climbed into one of the wagons.

Fredericksburg was a skeleton of the city it had been. The few buildings that were not completely burned out served as hospitals. Wounded soldiers lay under trees, on wooden sidewalks, under wagons. Ambulances stood idle. Untreated men lay dying.

"Why aren't these men being treated?" Clara demanded. "Who is in charge?"

Clara's questions were met by blank looks. Men were dying, yet no one seemed to care. There was only one thing to do.

Getting a wagon, Clara raced back to Belle Plain. She boarded a steamer for Washington. That night, she was pounding on the door of Henry Wilson, chairman of the Senate's Military Committee.

"Senator, something must be done at Fredericksburg. Men

are dying for lack of treatment, supplies, and medicine. Can't you do something?"

"Of course I can, Miss Barton!"

By ten o'clock that evening the quartermaster general and his staff climbed aboard a waiting steamer. The next day, order was returning to Fredericksburg. The city was a new place when Clara returned three days later. Every soldier was being treated.

"We owe you everything," one captain told Clara. "You have saved so many lives."

Clara shook her head. "It is God we must thank," she murmured. "Remember Psalm 46:1: 'God is our refuge and strength, a very present help in trouble.' Let us pray that this trouble will end soon."

In March 1865, Abraham Lincoln was again sworn in as president. With the war drawing to a close, Clara had a new project in mind. She took her idea to Henry Wilson.

"Senator, these letters are from people all over the United States." Clara dumped two large bundles onto the senator's desk. "They have been addressed to me, I suppose, because of my connection with the war. Each letter asks a question. 'Where is my brother?' 'Have you heard of my son?' 'Can you help me find news of my husband?' Senator, I cannot answer these letters because I do not have the answers. But with the government's help, I think I could find them."

"Clara, the government has suffered a great expense from this war. You must—"

"I realize that many of these people have paid a very high price as well, Senator. Can you imagine the sadness these people feel? They want to know. They deserve to know."

Senator Wilson stared at the letters.

"You wish to undertake this job, Clara? Don't you feel you might use a rest?"

"Will these people be able to rest until they have their answers? Senator, this job needs to be done. I am willing to start right away, with your permission."

"This will take more than my permission. I will have to talk to the president."

President Lincoln was quick to agree with Clara. He sent her to Annapolis to set up a station.

On April 3, Robert E. Lee surrendered his troops to General Grant. The last cannon had sounded. The war was over. But on April 14, a final shot plunged the country into grief. President Lincoln had been killed.

In Annapolis, letters flooded the tent Clara was using. Records were checked and double-checked. Information drifted in. Clara made a list of missing men. She hoped to have it printed and distributed across the country. Then anyone with information about a missing person could contact her.

Printers told Clara that the list was too big to print. In desperation, she sent a letter to President Andrew Johnson. She prayed he would see the value of her work.

On the day he received Clara's letter, President Johnson sat down at his desk. He wrote: *Let this printing be done as speedily as possible, consistent with the public interest.*

With the lists of missing men printed, Clara arranged them according to states. She sent them to newspapers and hospitals. The response was quick.

Letters came from all over the country. Released prisoners,

wounded men in hospitals, and officers scribbled down information. Often the listed men were dead, but sometimes the
men were in another part of the country. Pieces in the giant
jigsaw puzzle slid into place. But one large piece was still
missing.

"What happened to the soldiers at the Confederate prison
in Andersonville?" Clara asked. "That prison in Georgia held
thousands of captives."

The answer came from a surprising source.

"My name is Dorrence Atwater, Miss Barton. I believe I
can help you."

Clara stared at the young man before her desk. His wrinkled face made him look old.

"How can you help us, Mr. Atwater? Please take a seat."

As the man collapsed into a chair, he handed a bundle of
papers to Clara.

"I'm from Connecticut, Miss Barton. I enlisted when I
was about sixteen. Those Rebs captured a bunch of us and
took us to Andersonville. It was awful. They treated us like
animals." The man's voice rose in anger.

"But how did you get these names?"

"A fever came along and started killin' off the prisoners.
Killed some of the Confederates, too. I had it bad for awhile,
but somehow I got rid of it. When I got so I could see again,
the guards put me into the surgeon's tent. Told me to keep a
list for them of the dying. Each time a prisoner died, I had to
write his name, date of death, and his regiment."

"Didn't the surgeon keep the list? How did you get this?"

"I made two lists. Tied one copy into my coat lining.
Thought someone might want it someday. Read about you and

what you were doin'. Thought you might be the one."

Clara leafed through the pages. There were thousands of names.

"Mr. Atwater, you have done a wonderful thing. You not only have done a great service for your country, but you will also answer the questions of thousands of families."

The man smiled. "I'm glad that I could do something to help out those fellows. That Andersonville prison was an awful place, Miss Barton."

"I know." Clara sighed. "One more thing, Mr. Atwater. Where were these men buried?"

"In the field at Andersonville. Guess there must be over ten thousand of 'em."

"And the graves, Mr. Atwater. Are they marked?"

"Nope. But that list has them recorded in the order they died, Miss Barton."

"Do you suppose if we went to Andersonville, you could help me put up markers for these men?

"I know you would probably hate to go back there, Mr. Atwater, but it would be so comforting to the families."

The man looked at the floor. Clara could understand his reluctance to go to the place where he had suffered so much.

"I see what you mean, Miss Barton. If you like, I'll go back with you."

Through the summer of 1865, Dorrence Atwater and Clara worked under a blazing sun. Each grave at Andersonville was marked. By fall, Clara had convinced Secretary of War Stanton to turn the Andersonville graveyard into a national cemetery.

Clara was anxious to get back to her work in Annapolis. When she returned, however, bad news waited.

"We're out of money," one of the staff members announced.

Clara knew the government didn't have much money to give her. She had used her own savings, but that too was gone. Letters waited to be answered. More lists had to be distributed. The staff had to be paid.

"If only there were some way I could raise money," Clara said to a friend.

"You could talk," the friend suggested.

"What do you mean?"

"Clara, people would pay to hear you speak. You could tell them about the war, about your adventures."

"That's an idea. Perhaps I'd be able to locate more of our missing men."

It didn't take long to set up a series of lectures. The name "Clara Barton" appeared on signs in Indiana, Iowa, Illinois, Ohio, and Michigan. Old soldiers surrounded her to thank her for helping them. And after each lecture, Clara sent the money she received back to Annapolis.

By 1868, almost twenty-three thousand missing soldiers had been located. Clara closed the final record book at Annapolis and decided to continue lecturing.

But as she spoke in Portland, Maine, Clara lost her voice. Unable to continue, she walked off the stage.

"You need to rest, Clara," her doctor said. "You have been so busy with everyone else, you haven't been taking care of yourself. I suggest you take a rest for two or three years."

"But must I give up lecturing?"

"Of course. Why don't you go to Europe?"

Following her doctor's orders, Clara sailed for Europe in September 1869.

After a restful voyage, Clara unloaded her bags in Scotland. From there she went to London, then Paris, and finally to Geneva, Switzerland.

Throwing open her window one morning, Clara saw a carriage pull up. Several gentlemen stepped out and walked into the house.

Soon a knock came at her door.

"Miss Barton, there are some gentlemen to see you."

Clara went to meet her visitors.

"We're here as representatives of the International Convention of Geneva, Miss Barton," Dr. Appia said. "We've come to ask your country's help."

"I'm not sure I understand."

"Our organization has been trying to persuade the United States to join us in promoting the Red Cross."

"The Red Cross? I'm afraid I am not familiar with the group."

"Its purpose is to help the wounded in war and people like yourself who are working in army hospitals. Any hospital flying this flag would be neutral and could not be captured."

Dr. Appia stood and unfurled a folded cloth. On a white background stood a deep red cross.

"It's beautiful, Dr. Appia," Clara exclaimed. "Your organization sounds interesting. It would be wonderful to have hospitals out of danger."

"Not only hospitals, but medical supplies that are being

taken to hospitals as well."

"You say the United States is not interested?" Clara asked.

"We have asked several times. They refuse to sign."

"The war in my country was a terrible thing. We are still recovering."

"I know, Miss Barton. I was a doctor in Italy when Napoleon sent his troops. War is terrible. But it is even worse when the injured cannot be treated, when doctors and nurses fear being captured, when medicines are destroyed."

"The Red Cross interests me," Clara said. "I would like to know more about it."

"I shall leave these things with you." Dr. Appia took a pile of pamphlets and clippings from his briefcase and set them on the nearest table.

After the gentlemen left, Clara read the material.

"Your organization sounds like a true help to countries in war," she later told Dr. Appia.

"It is good to hear you say that, Miss Barton. We feel such an organization could be very important in war. And the Red Cross is getting prepared for action. Things look very bad between Prussia and France."

Dr. Appia was right. Two weeks later, the cannons of Germany and France sounded. War had come to Europe. Clara would see the Red Cross in action.

Dr. Appia encouraged Clara to go to Basle, the Swiss town where the Red Cross was headquartered during the war. She agreed.

Clara was impressed by what she saw. Doctors and nurses worked hard. Each day, wagons brought fresh medicine and bandages. The wounded had plenty of food. The hospitals were packed with wounded men, but everything was organized.

"It's marvelous!" Clara exclaimed to a nurse one day. "No matter how fierce the battle grows, you take good care of the wounded. America must learn of the Red Cross."

Clara decided to see the Red Cross working at the battlefront. She packed her bags and headed for Strasbourg, a French town being torn apart by German armies.

Clara was asked to take a group of Americans to safety. She would have to go through German lines.

"I will go!" Clara answered. "God will help me."

The people piled into a wagon, pushing and shouting. Clara had trouble getting them quiet.

"We will have to pass through German lines," she said. "Because you are Americans, you will be safe. But please let me talk to the guards."

Clara took the American flag she had been given by the doctors at Strasbourg. They told her to show it at each German post.

At the first post, a guard marched up beside the wagon. Clara lifted the American flag so he could see it.

"What is that?" he shouted.

"Why. . .why, it's the American flag," Clara stammered.

"I don't believe you. Hand it to me."

The soldier pulled it out of Clara's hands and stalked off. After several minutes, he returned.

"This is not the American flag. I was in America. I looked at this flag under a good light just to be sure. You are under arrest!"

"But you're making a mistake," Clara argued. "Where did you go in America?"

"Mostly in Mexico."

"They have their own flag. Isn't there some way you can check this?"

"All right, I shall see if this flag is listed in the books we have." Once again, the guard marched away.

Clara turned to the people in the wagon. Many were crying. "Please do not worry. We will get through."

When the guard returned, he threw the flag in Clara's face.

"I have checked. You may go on. But you are fortunate to have received such kind treatment here."

Clara slapped the reins. As the wagon jerked forward, her passengers cheered.

Clara began thinking of the guard's words. What would happen the next time they were stopped?

An idea flashed through her mind. Clara handed the reins to the man sitting beside her. She got out a needle and thread. Untying the red ribbon from her collar, she formed a cross on her handkerchief. Hastily she sewed it on the sleeve of her dress.

As the wagon lumbered into the next stop, a guard ran up. When he saw the red cross on her dress, he told Clara to move on.

As the war continued, Clara saw thousands of people helped by the Red Cross. The war stopped, but the Red Cross kept on. It planned how to rebuild damaged areas.

Clara sailed for home, anxious to bring the Red Cross to America.

Clara had gotten little rest in Europe. Once she arrived in America, she traveled to a small rest home in Dansville, New

York. She would have to be strong before she started fighting for the Red Cross. The fresh air and good food soon made Clara feel much better.

In 1877, Clara stood before President Rutherford B. Hayes. She gave him a letter from the president of the International Red Cross.

"Mr. President, surely you see the value of such an organization. We all hope that war never comes again, but we should be prepared if it does."

President Hayes looked up at Clara. "Miss Barton, I respect your interest in this matter. But don't you feel we would be getting involved with countries far away? It seems to me we should be interested in keeping our own country stable."

"But can't we do both?" Clara argued. "Our world is growing smaller. A man is working on a machine through which we can talk to people miles away. It may work."

"And it may not—just like this Red Cross. A small machine takes only a few dollars to build. But your plan would call for a large amount of money."

"And what is the price of a human life, Sir? I have seen the Red Cross save thousands of lives."

President Hayes smiled. "Miss Barton, I suggest you take your letter to the secretary of state. See what he has to say."

The secretary of state agreed with the president. He sent Clara to the assistant secretary of state. Again she was disappointed. But Clara was determined to bring the Red Cross to her country.

In 1880, James Garfield became president. He was a friend of Clara's from the war.

"Surely you recall the horrible days of battle, Mr.

President," Clara said to him. "Please read this letter and see if you don't find value in the Red Cross."

Clara watched President Garfield read the letter. He returned the letter and shook her hand.

"Those battlefields were sights I can never forget, Miss Barton. I remember a boy who was shot as he stood just a few inches from me."

"I saw many boys like that," Clara said.

"Miss Barton, I like this plan. Naturally, you will have to see the secretary of state. He must have his say on matters involving other countries."

Clara looked down.

"Now, Miss Barton, I mean what I say. I do like this plan. I will relay to Secretary Blaine my feelings. He will expect you, and I'm sure you two will get along fine."

Secretary Blaine welcomed Clara warmly. He too liked the idea.

It had taken almost five years, but Clara had convinced the officials of her country to believe in the Red Cross program.

The Red Cross treaty sped through Congress. Everywhere people were talking about the new organization. Once the president signed the treaty, Clara could officially begin making plans.

President Garfield called her to the White House.

"Surely, you will become the first president of the Red Cross," Clara said. "It's an honor due you as head of the country."

"No, it is an honor due you for the work you have done. Without you, there would be no Red Cross. You must organize and lead the group."

Sixty-five-year-old Clara accepted the new job.

That July, as Clara was riding in a carriage, she noticed people running. She asked the driver to stop. Stepping down from the carriage, Clara stopped a woman who was crying.

"What's wrong?" Clara asked.

"It's the president. He's been shot!"

Clara climbed into her carriage and ordered the driver to return home. She prayed for the president's recovery.

For months, the president lingered between life and death. But on September 19, 1881, President Garfield died.

Sadly, Clara returned to Dansville. Her hopes for an American Red Cross dimmed. Wasn't this the role the Lord had chosen for her? Had she failed Him?

Within weeks, Clara had the answer. The new president, Chester Arthur, invited her to the White House.

"President Garfield told me of the plans for the Red Cross, Miss Barton. I see no reason these plans should not be carried out."

Clara could almost hear the words of Mark 4:40: *"Why are ye so fearful? how is it that ye have no faith?"*

Newspapers soon criticized Clara. Many people thought it was wrong for a woman to have so much publicity. "This Barton person is merely seeking to make herself famous," wrote one editor. "This is a man's work," observed another.

But on July 26, 1882, the United States joined the International Red Cross. The American Red Cross soon blazed into action.

A forest fire raged across Michigan. People were homeless and starving. An urgent plea for help reached the American Red Cross. Clara saw that the plea was answered. Soon letters of gratitude poured in:

> *Dear Miss Barton,*
> *We lost our whole farm in the fire. All our stock was*
> *killed. If it had not been for the help you sent us, we*
> *could never have survived. God bless you, dear*
> *saint. We are now building our house again. We will*
> *make it, thanks to you.*
>
> > *Forever your servant,*
> > *Hannah Mills*

Julian B. Hubbell, a medical student, offered his services as a field agent for the Red Cross. His family was wealthy. He requested no salary. "My payment will come from being useful to so humane and Christian an organization as the Red Cross," he said. Clara accepted his offer.

Clara soon heard from an old friend, Benjamin Butler. As a Union general, he had supported Clara on the battlefields. Now he was governor of Massachusetts. He invited Clara to visit him. She went at once.

"You have probably heard of the efforts of Miss Dorothea Dix to improve the lot of those unfortunates in our country's prisons," the old general began. "I'm hoping you might help us with such an effort here in Massachusetts."

"Me?" Clara exclaimed. "But I know nothing about prisons."

"You know a great deal about humane treatment and service to others. I would like you to serve as superintendent of the Women's Reformatory Prison at Sherborn."

Give me your direction, O God, she prayed. *Is this a*

path You would have me follow? For several minutes she was silent.

"If you think it is a job I can do," she said to the governor, "I will accept. But I must insist that I maintain my duties with the Red Cross."

Governor Butler agreed.

In the prison, Clara brought the same kindness she had shown on the battlefields. Each day she visited with the prisoners. A complaint box was put up so the inmates could express themselves.

One guest was amazed that the prisoners could freely visit Clara's office.

"Surely you are too easy with these people," the friend complained. "You are a good Christian woman. Why would you wish to expose yourself to contact with the likes of such individuals?"

Clara smiled. "I thank you for calling me a good Christian woman. I return the compliment twofold, as I have great respect for you. Yet I am surprised that you would raise such a question."

"Surprised? I am sure others would feel the same as I do. The governor undoubtedly recognizes your gift for organization and efficiency, qualities not often given a woman. But surely he does not expect you to have personal visits with the prisoners."

Clara listened, feeling amused and annoyed. Finally she could not restrain herself.

"Governor Butler has given me responsibility for this institution to handle as I deem necessary. To visit personally with the inmates is hardly a torture. If I am not mistaken, one of

Jesus' final actions was a promise to a prisoner who suffered the same agonizing death as He did. You haven't forgotten, have you?"

The visitor's gaze fell to the floor.

Clara did everything at the prison. She joined the cooks in the kitchen, stretching limited food supplies. She kept the financial records, working long into the night to cut expenses. She fought for new sewing machines and then set up sewing classes.

One of her favorite activities was talking with the prisoners each morning in the chapel. "There are mistakes in my life, just as there are mistakes in yours," Clara told the women. "Yet we are all blessed with the same God, who is merciful and forgiving. We can turn to Him anywhere, at any time."

The prisoners listened to Clara. They accepted her as their friend. One inmate wrote home to her family:

Miss Barton gives us hope in tomorrow. I know the Lord must have sent her here. Each day she tells us about someone else who was reclaimed by the Lord. I am going to see her in the morning. She takes special concern about those of us who have large families. She is one grand woman!

Clara was satisfied with the changes she brought to the prison. But she missed being close to the Red Cross. When she requested a release from her duties, Governor Butler agreed.

"In less than a year, you accomplished what it would have taken anyone else a lifetime to achieve," he told her. "But then, it was no more than I expected from a woman like yourself."

Rains pelted the Pennsylvania mountains. The Conemaugh River became an angry snake. But the thirty thousand people of Johnstown felt safe. They were protected by a strong dam.

On May 31, 1889, the dam broke. Deadly waters poured into Johnstown. Within hours, four thousand people were swept away in the water. Houses were pulled from their foundations. The call for help went out.

Clara did not waste a moment. By the first week in June, she was on the scene, wading in mud up to her waist and shouting instructions to Red Cross volunteers.

"This is no place for a lady," General Hastings, the military commander, told her. "We have not recovered all the missing bodies."

"We are here to assist you, General," Clara answered firmly. "We will not be getting in your way, but we might be able to help clear your path."

General Hastings discovered that Clara meant exactly that. Setting up her headquarters in a deserted railroad car, she rolled into action.

Clara set up places for handing out donations. Clothing, food, tools, bedding, furniture, and other supplies poured in from around the nation.

Soup kitchens were set up. Men, women, and children gathered in giant tents to share hot food and news of neighbors.

Carloads of lumber arrived from Illinois and Iowa. Volunteers built homes.

Mr. and Mrs. John Tittle proved to be two of Clara's best helpers. They had a frightening story to tell.

"The flood tore us right out of our home," Mr. Tittle explained. "Thankfully, we were together and held hands over the ridgepole of our house as we floated down the river."

"Every time I felt like giving up and letting go, I felt John's hands clasp mine harder," his wife said. "I just kept praying, hoping, and praying some more."

"Someone must have been listening to your prayers," Clara said.

"That's what we believe," John Tittle declared. "Our house floated all the way down to Kernville, where it got hooked onto the bridge. Would you believe that even our dog and parrot were alive inside?"

Mrs. Tittle looked up. "That's why we've come to you, Miss Barton. We prayed that the Lord might spare us. Well, we're here all right, and we'd like to thank Him by helping others."

Clara nodded. "We can use you. There is much to be done."

Although the flood had swept away homes and property, nothing could carry off the spirit of the people. Johnstown began to rebuild. Within weeks, businesses and shops opened. School was held in tents, then moved into actual classrooms.

Once the people were on their feet, the Red Cross needed to leave. "The key to our success is that we appear only as emergency relief and help," Clara told audiences. "Our goal is to provide necessary assistance, to help organize work efforts, to share the donations of others with those who need it most. Never must we be taken as intruders or trespassers. Help and get out—that is our goal."

A cool breeze blew across the harbor in Havana.

"Sure you wouldn't like to go below deck, Miss Barton?" a crewman suggested. "A little old lady like yourself shouldn't be standing out here catching cold."

Clara straightened. "Young man, I would recommend you to go below deck yourself. There is quite enough wind already without you adding your own."

At seventy-six, Clara was not interested in anyone worrying about her health. It was 1898, and the Spanish had squelched a rebellion by the Cubans. A Cuban request for help reached the United States, and President McKinley had called on Clara.

"What ship might that be?" Clara asked, pointing across the harbor.

"It's the *Maine,*" the crewman answered.

But Clara was far more interested in people. Once she reached shore, she headed directly to the hospitals. What she found shocked her.

Cuban men, women, and children injured in the fighting with Spain lay on floors. Dead bodies remained among the living. Stomachs were bloated from malnutrition.

"The first thing we must do is feed these poor, starving creatures," Clara declared. Quickly, she pinned up her floor-length skirts.

"Hardly ladylike!" a nurse murmured.

"There will be many times to be a lady," Clara shot back. "At present, it serves our purposes more if I am able to move swiftly."

Clara turned warehouses into giant food kitchens. For the first time in months, patients were given plenty of good food.

On February 13, Clara was working at her writing table in Havana. Suddenly the room shook. The veranda door burst open, revealing a blaze of light.

"It's the *Maine!*" a voice in the hallway shouted. "They've blown up the *Maine!*"

"Merciful God," Clara prayed, "please help us."

Tension filled the air. Were the Spanish responsible for blowing up the *Maine*? People talked of war.

But Clara had no time for such talk. When officials from Washington arrived, she took them to the worst spots on the island. At Artemisa, thousands of Cubans without food and homes roamed aimlessly.

"This is not the worst of it," Clara said. "We have already lost three thousand from starvation and inadequate care."

"Do what you must do," the officials told Clara. "We shall carry the word back home, and you shall receive support."

Clara became a human hurricane, seeing that new hospitals were set up in warehouses, supervising food rationing, getting Cuban officials to enforce new laws. Food, clothing, medicine, and bedding were shipped from the United States.

On April 25, 1898, war was declared between the United States and Spain. Fearing for her volunteers, Clara moved Red Cross headquarters to Tampa, Florida.

Some Washington officials were afraid supplies might end up in enemy hands. Clara persuaded officials that her work was essential. President McKinley ordered all government agencies and offices to give full recognition to the Red Cross and to use its services.

Jubilant, Clara headed back into action. Loaded with vital supplies, the *State of Texas* sailed to Cuba.

The *State of Texas* anchored in Guantanamo, where the U.S. Marines were in control. An urgent request came for Clara to journey to the battlefront.

"She's in her seventies," one physician argued. "We can't ask her to travel so close to the fighting."

"You don't know Clara Barton," another official said. "That is where she feels most at home."

The decision was made. Clara left for the front in a hay wagon.

"It will be a bumpy ride," the driver told her.

"All I care about is arriving safely," she answered.

Clara found three giant tents with operating tables, surrounded by smaller tents for the wounded soldiers. Men lay in soaking grass. The sun blazed down on them during the daytime, while chilly dew covered them at night.

Clara headed first to the cookhouse. She built a fireplace and ordered big kettles scrubbed and cleaned. Then she began making gruel. The aroma caused the wounded to cry out.

"Miss Barton is here! We'll get some decent food."

She had no blankets, so Clara tore strips of muslin to cover the patients. She saw that the wounded received her famous "Red Cross cider," made from stewed apples, prunes, and lime juice.

One night, as Clara helped a surgeon operate, a shot rang out. Clara felt a body lean against her. She lowered the staff member's body to the ground. His bullet wound was fatal. Clara closed the man's eyes, tears coming to her own. She removed the body from the area. Then she returned to her position at the operating table.

More Red Cross volunteers joined Clara in Cuba. But

an outbreak of yellow fever added new problems. Officials feared people would spread the disease. Clara, recognizing the importance of supplies reaching the starving people in Santiago, insisted on sailing to shore.

Clara continued directing Red Cross services in Cuba. By the time she sailed for home in November 1899, her organization had distributed six thousand tons of supplies.

"When history books record the American victory over Spain in this campaign," President McKinley wrote Clara, "you deserve mention among our finest soldiers."

CHAPTER 8

With a firm hand, Clara signed her name. She folded the document and slid it into an envelope. "There, it is done," she murmured softly.

Clara leaned back in her chair. She knew about the arguing within the American Red Cross.

"She's just too old, too demanding."

"It wouldn't be so bad, but she's so bossy. Everything must be done her way."

Some people felt Clara was no longer the right person to be running the American Red Cross. At eighty-four, she had held the position for twenty-three years.

"Do you have any mail to go out today?" A young girl stood at the doorway.

"Yes," Clara answered, holding up the envelope. "Indeed I do."

Newspaper headlines carried the story of Clara Barton's resignation as president of the American Red Cross. She wrote to her nephew Stephen:

I am the last of my generation—I am strange among the new. We cannot comprehend each other. I have lacked the knowledge of the newer generation, and done my work badly, and naturally grow discouraged and timid and want to escape it all. . . .

Stephen hurried to Clara's home. She enjoyed his visits. He encouraged her to share stories from her childhood. Eagerly she wrote *The Story of My Childhood* for young readers.

One afternoon, Clara sat in the garden enjoying the sunset. She heard a noise behind her. Turning, she saw a stranger approaching.

"Miss Barton? Is it really you?"

Clara stared at the man. His hair was white and shaggy. His brown suit was faded and worn. But there was something familiar about him. "I'm sorry. I don't seem able to remember your name."

"I wouldn't expect you to, Miss Barton. Guess you just knew me by Pete. It was a long time ago."

"Pete!" Clara exclaimed. "I remember. It was at Harpers Ferry. You drove the wagon to Harpers Ferry. We had to travel by night so we could pass the other wagons. Yes, I do remember. You were about the best driver I'd ever seen."

Pete sat down on the bench beside Clara. "It was about fifty years ago, Miss Barton. It's amazing that you would remember me."

"I will never forget those days."

Pete pulled out a crumpled scrap of paper from his coat and handed it to Clara.

"I want you to have this, Miss Barton. I got it from my son while he was in Cuba a few years ago during the Spanish-American War. Thought you might like to read it."

"You read it to me, Pete. My eyes are not as good as they once were."

"Glad to, Miss Barton."

He read:

Dear Dad,

Just wanted you to know I am safe here and feeling fine. I'm getting rid of this fever fast. The fighting is letting up, and I think I'll be coming home soon.

By the way, Dad, you know that Miss Clara Barton you always talk about from your war days? Well, would you believe she's down here in Cuba? She moves faster than anybody else, and she's even made the food eatable. They still call her the "angel of the battlefield." I can understand why!

That's about all for now, Dad. Take good care of yourself.

Your son,
Richard

"It's a lovely letter," Clara said.

"He's a fine boy, Miss Barton. Lives right next door to me. Never given me a bad moment—not like so many young folks these days."

"It is a changing world, isn't it, Pete?"

"You haven't changed much, Miss Barton. Still small and feisty, aren't you?"

Clara shook her head. "Small, perhaps, but not quite as feisty. I feel the years, Pete."

He smiled. "Some days, I do. But I'm reminded of the words of the good book, Miss Barton. Remember Job 42:12? 'So the LORD blessed the latter end of Job more than his beginning.' And Proverbs 16:31: 'The hoary head is a crown of glory.' "

Clara sat in silence. For so long, the troubles of the Red Cross had filled her mind. She had allowed the worries of this world to weigh her down.

Clara took Pete's hand. "You have been a welcome visitor, good friend. Surely the Lord directed your footsteps to me. Now, I baked a fresh apple pie this morning. Would you stay and help me eat it?"

"Will there be any Red Cross cider to wash it down with?" Pete asked, his eyes teasing.

"We shall look," Clara answered.

Slowly, the two of them walked into the house, stopping to glance up at the red, white, and blue of the United States flag, and at the red cross on the white banner flying overhead.

"Make sure you tie that securely, Miss Barton," the gardener said.

Clara tied the plant bud carefully. She rose to her feet and dusted off her skirt.

At eighty-nine, Clara was taking on a new challenge. She was learning how to graft trees. That same month—April 1911—she'd finished writing *The History of the Red Cross*.

"There are too many people who act ninety when they are but fifty," Clara wrote to a friend. "I, too, feel the pains and aches of age, but there is still much to do before I go to meet my loving Creator."

Clara wrote her will and drew up instructions for her funeral. Her horse, Baba, was to be sent to a friend in Virginia.

Clara surrounded herself with books. She enjoyed the Greek stories of victories over great odds.

"Perhaps you enjoy reading of such conquests since

you had so many battles of your own," her friend, Dr. Julian Hubbell, observed.

Clara shook her head. "My battles were small. How often I think of those boys on the bloody battlefields. Many of them uttered no complaint, yet they lay in mortal pain."

In July, a box arrived. It was a surprise gift from an unknown admirer.

"Oh, my!" Clara exclaimed when she opened the box. "It's a typewriter. I have no idea how such a machine works."

"If I know you, you will learn with great speed," Dr. Hubbell said.

"I shall give it my best," Clara said.

She studied the directions carefully. Within two hours, she finished a typewritten letter. "You must pardon the mistakes," she pleaded. "The meeting of an old woman and a young machine does not always lead to favorable results."

Autumn brought pain, but Clara's spirits rallied as Christmas approached.

"I am feeling much better today," she told a reporter in mid-December, "and have every hope of spending a pleasant and joyful Christmas when I shall celebrate my ninetieth birthday."

Clara did enjoy her birthday. Friends and relatives visited. As Clara gazed across the room at a small nativity scene, her lined face brightened.

"Would you believe there are those who feel sorry for us who must share our birthdays with the Savior?" she asked. "What greater joy could one ask for a birthday?"

With the new year, Clara sensed her life was ending. In a final letter to her friend, the Grand Duchess of Baden, Clara said farewell:

Dearest, dearest Grand Duchess,
They tell me I am changing worlds, and one of my
last thoughts and wishes is to tell you of my
unchanging love and devotion to you. I have waited
long to be able to tell you of better news, but it does
not come.

Thanks, oh, thanks for your letters and your love.
Dr. Hubbell will write you of me when I am gone
and I commend him to you. May God bless and keep
you forever more.

Blessings ever,
Clara Barton

April came with the joyful tidings of Easter. On April 10, Clara had a dream that brought Dr. Hubbell and her nephew Stephen to her bedside. She sat up, her back braced against pillows.

"I thought I was on the battlefield," Clara said. "The poor boys were lying on the cold ground with no nurses and no physicians to do anything for them. I saw surgeons coming, and too much was needed by all of them to give special attention to anyone. Then I woke to hear myself groan because I have a stupid pain in my back. Here on a good bed with every attention! I am ashamed that I murmur!"

Clara had little time left for murmuring. On April 12, 1912, with Dr. Hubbell and Stephen beside her, she said her last words. "Let me go!"

News of Clara Barton's death captured newspaper headlines around the world. In keeping with her wishes, the funeral ceremony was simple.

Clara's body was taken back to Massachusetts for burial.

Dr. Hubbell and Stephen hired a covered express wagon for part of the journey.

"It's a sorry night for such a mission," the wagon driver remarked, peering through the thick fog. "Will you be taking the lady far?"

"Miss Barton is to be buried in North Oxford, Massachusetts," Dr. Hubbell replied quietly.

"Is this the body of Clara Barton?" the driver exclaimed. "Why, my father was a Confederate soldier, and at the battle of Antietam he was wounded in the neck and was bleeding to death when Miss Barton found him and bound up his wounds."

Soldiers waited at the city of Worcester, Massachusetts, to accompany the body to Oxford. Veterans, friends, and relatives gathered to share their stories of Clara. As her body was buried beside the graves of her mother and father, the song "Jesus, Lover of My Soul" carried along the warm spring breezes:

Jesus, lover of my soul, Let me to Thy bosom fly,
While the nearer waters roll, While the tempest still
is high!
Hide me, O my Savior, hide, Till the storm of life
is past;
Safe into the haven guide, O receive my soul at last!

Other refuge have I none—Hangs my helpless soul
on Thee;
Leave, O, leave me not alone, Still support and
comfort me!
All my trust on Thee is stayed, All my help from
Thee I bring;

*Cover my defenseless head, With the shadow of
    Thy wing.*
*Thou, O Christ, art all I want, More than all in
    Thee I find;*
*Raise the fallen, cheer the faint, Heal the sick and
    lead the blind.*
*Just and holy is Thy Name: I am all
    unrighteousness;*
*False and full of sin I am, Thou art full of truth
    and grace.*

*Plenteous grace with Thee is found, Grace to cover
    all my sin;*
*Let the healing streams abound, Make and keep me
    pure within.*
*Thou of life the fountain art, Freely let me take
    of Thee;*
Spring Thou up within my heart, Rise to all eternity.

If you enjoyed

AMERICAN HEROES,

check out these other great
Backpack Books!